JESUS

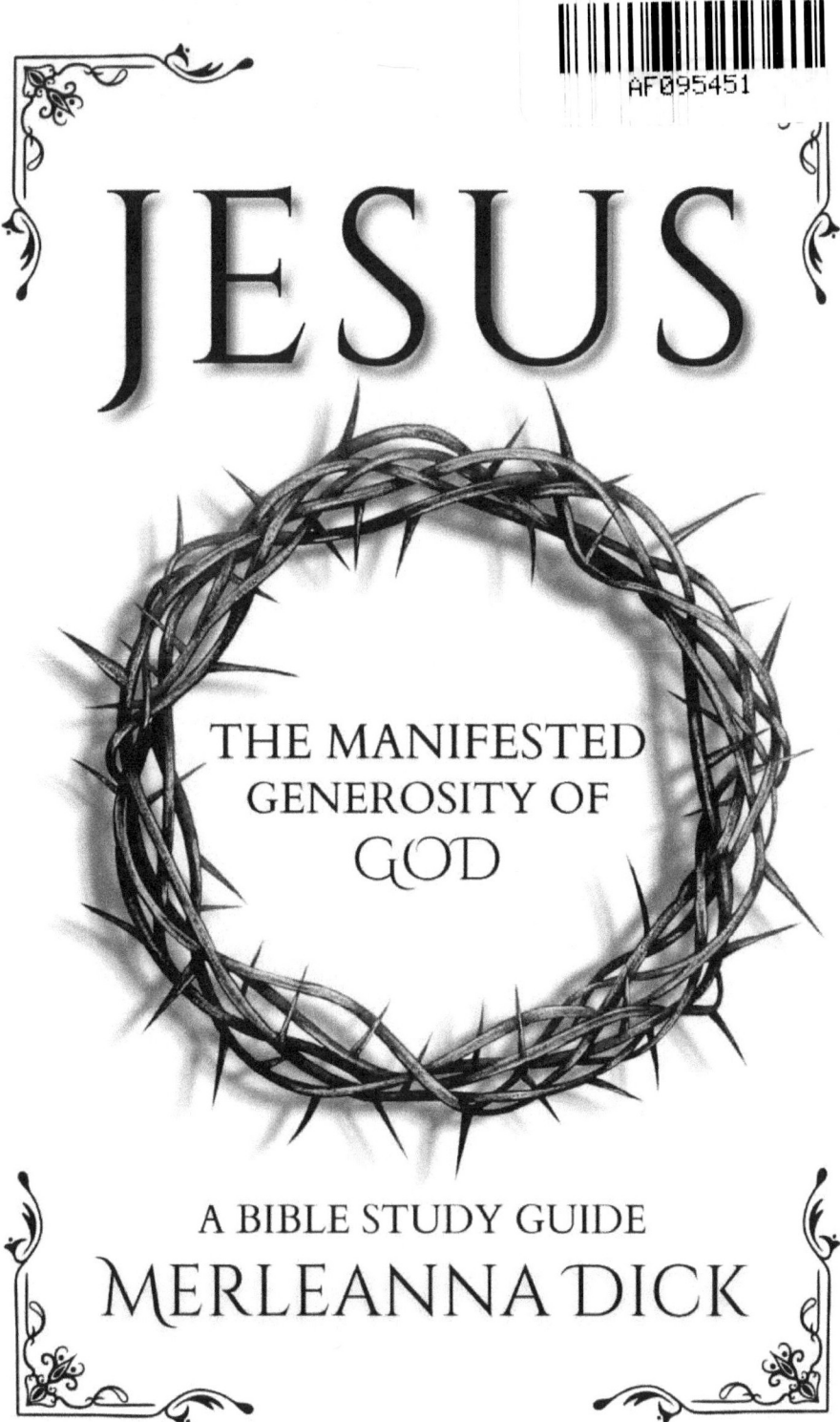

THE MANIFESTED
GENEROSITY OF
GOD

A BIBLE STUDY GUIDE
MERLEANNA DICK

JESUS

THE MANIFESTED GENEROSITY OF GOD

A BIBLE STUDY GUIDE

Jesus the Manifested Generosity of God

Copyright © 2024 by Merleanna Dick

Printed in the United States of America

ISBN: 9798218483197

Published by Joseph's Ministry, LLC

(www.josephsministryllc.com)

Scriptures are taken from the Holy Bible, New International Version®, NIV®. Copyright © 1973, 1978, 1984, 2011 by Biblica, Inc.™ Used by permission of Zondervan. All rights reserved worldwide.

Scripture quotations marked (GNT) are from the Good News Translation in Today's English Version- Second Edition Copyright © 1992 by American Bible Society. Used by Permission.

Scripture quotations marked (NKJV) are taken from the NEW KING JAMES VERSION®. Copyright© 1982 by Thomas Nelson, Inc. Used by permission. All rights reserved.

Scripture quotations are from the ESV® Bible (The Holy Bible, English Standard Version®), © 2001 by Crossway, a publishing ministry of Good News Publishers. Used by permission. All rights reserved. The ESV text may not be quoted in any publication made available to the public by a Creative Commons license. The ESV may not be translated in whole or in part into any other language.

Scripture quotations marked (NLT) are taken from the Holy Bible, New Living Translation, copyright ©1996, 2004, 2015 by Tyndale House Foundation. Used by permission of Tyndale House Publishers, Carol Stream, Illinois 60188. All rights reserved.

Scripture quotations marked (KJV) are taken from the KING JAMES VERSION, public domain.

Scripture quotations marked MSG are taken from THE MESSAGE, copyright © 1993, 2002, 2018 by Eugene H. Peterson. Used by permission of NavPress, represented by Tyndale House Publishers. All rights reserved.

Scripture quotations marked (HCSB) are taken from the HOLMAN CHRISTIAN STANDARD BIBLE, Copyright© 1999, 2000, 2002, 2003 by Holman Bible Publishers, Nashville Tennessee. All rights reserved.

Scripture quotations marked (ICB) are taken from the INTERNATIONAL CHILDREN'S BIBLE®. Copyright© 1986, 1988, 1999 by Thomas Nelson, Inc. Used by permission. All rights reserved.

Scripture quotations marked (TLB) are taken from The Living Bible copyright © 1971. Used by permission of Tyndale House Publishers, Carol Stream, Illinois 60188. All rights reserved.

Taken from the Holy Bible: Easy-to-Read Version (ERV), International Edition © 2013, 2016 by Bible League International and used by permission.

Scripture is taken from GOD'S WORD®. © 1995, 2003, 2013, 2014, 2019, 2020 by God's Word to the Nations Mission Society. Used by permission.

Scripture quotations are from the EasyEnglish Bible Copyright © MissionAssist 2019 - Charitable Incorporated Organisation 1162807. Used by permission. All rights reserved."

All rights reserved. No part of this publication may be reproduced, distributed, or transmitted in any form or by any means, including photocopying, recording, or other electronic or mechanical methods, without the prior written permission of the author except in the case of brief quotations embodied in critical reviews and certain other noncommercial uses permitted by copyright law.

TABLE OF CONTENTS

ACKNOWLEDGEMENTS 1
FOREWORD 3
INTRODUCTION 5
    Why is this manual useful in connecting the OT and NT? 7
    How to use this manual? 8
CHAPTER 1 11
Jesus the Manifested Generosity of God..11
    Why is this gift God's generosity? Why is the Messiah Important? 11
    God's Plan.. 12
    The Life and Ministry of Jesus 14
    What was Jesus' Ministry on Earth?.. 15
    Jesus is called the Word 19
    Bible Reading Plan And Worksheet 22
        1st Month Bible Reading Assignment:................................. 22
        Scriptural Review:.. 22
        Terminology Research 23
CHAPTER 2 29
Bible Prophecy and the Messiah..29
    What does being the Messiah mean? 29
    What is prophecy and how do we recognize it in the Bible?...... 30
    How does Bible prophecy connect Jesus as the Messiah?.......... 32
    Bible Reading Plan And Worksheet 34
        2nd Month Bible Reading Assignment:................................ 34
        Scriptural Review:.. 34

  Terminology Research 35

CHAPTER 3 39

Messiah Paralleled in the OT and NT 39

 Parallel Scriptural Citations of Jesus Christ in the Bible 39

 Table 1 - Parallel Scriptural Citations of Jesus Christ in the Bible 40

 Biblical Cross-References of Old and New Covenants 51

 Table 2 - Biblical Cross-References of Old and New Covenants 52

 Bible Reading Plan And Worksheet 62

  3rd Month Bible Reading Assignment: 62

  Scriptural Review: 63

  Terminology Research 64

CHAPTER 4 67

Jesus's Mission on Earth 67

 Salvation 68

 Righteousness 70

 Healing 72

 Fellowship with God 73

 Bible Reading Plan And Worksheet 74

  4th Month Bible Reading Assignment: 74

  Scriptural Review: 75

  Terminology Research 78

CHAPTER 5 81

The Messiah and the Church 81

 Bible Reading Plan And Worksheet 84

  5th Month Bible Reading Assignment: 84

Scripture Review: 85

Terminology Research 87

CHAPTER 6 91

Jesus Christ A Prophet Like Moses 91

Moses 91

Jesus 92

How is Jesus a prophet like Moses and why is that important?.. 94

Bible Reading Plan And Worksheet 96

6th Month Bible Reading Assignment: 96

Scriptural Review: 96

Terminology Research 98

CHAPTER 7 101

Priest After the Order of Melchizedek 101

Bible Reading Plan And Worksheet 103

7th Month Bible Reading Assignment: 103

Scriptural Review: 104

Terminology Research 107

CHAPTER 8 111

The Nation of Israel is Important to Salvation 111

Jesus Christ the Son of God and the Seed of Abraham 113

Seed of Abraham and the Nation of Israel 114

God's Promise Fulfilled in Jesus – the Seed of Abraham 115

Bible Reading Plan And Worksheet 119

8th Month Bible Reading Assignment: 119

Scriptural Review: 119

Terminology Research 120

CHAPTER 9 125

Salvation and the Holy Spirit 125
    Three Baptisms 127
        John's Baptism to Repentance 127
        Jesus' Baptism to Salvation 128
        Holy Spirit's Baptism of Power 131
        Experience with the Trinity 132
    Bible Reading Plan And Worksheet 134
        9th Month Bible Reading Assignment: 134
        Scriptural Review: 134
        Terminology Research 136

CHAPTER 10 141
Worship God with Other Believers 141
    Why Worship God with Other Believers? 142
        (1) Show Love for One Another 143
        (2) Spiritual Growth and Encouragement 145
        (3) Celebrate God for Who He Is Together 146
    Bible Reading Plan And Worksheet 147
        10th Month Bible Reading Assignment: 147
        Scriptural Review: 148
        Terminology Research 148

CHAPTER 11 151
The Believer's Role in the Church Jesus Started 151
    (1) Worship Jesus Christ 152
    (2) Go and Make Disciples of all Humanity 153
    (3) Baptize Believers 154
    (4) Teach Believers to Keep Jesus' Command 155
    Ministry of Reconciliation 157

    Bible Reading Plan And Worksheet 157
        11th Month Bible Reading Assignment:............................. 157
        Scriptural Review:.. 158
        Terminology Research 159

CHAPTER 12 163

The Church's Role in the World 163

    Be Separate from the World... 164
    Show God's Image to the World... 166
    Show God's Love to One Another and Others 167
    Bible Reading Plan And Worksheet 168
        12th Month Bible Reading Assignment:............................. 168
        Scriptural Review:.. 169
        Terminology Research 170

CONCLUSION...173
WORK CITED..175
ADDITIONAL RESOURCES...177

    Bible Reading Plan.. 177
    Use a Bible Dictionary and/or Concordance............................ 177

ACKNOWLEDGEMENTS

First, I give honor to my Lord and Savior, Jesus Christ, without Whom I would not have an unshakable life. For it is in Him that I live, navigate through, and have success in life. His written and living Word, Jesus Christ, has revolutionized or transformed me into a confident person and bold witness for Him. His presence with me daily is what empowers me to be an overcomer over the schemes of the enemy, Satan. Lastly, God's faithfulness is the help I need when troubles come which are inevitable for this life. All these have been the things that have helped me become the person I am today. For this, I am eternally grateful.

I thank my husband, Ibinabo Natebo Dick, Sr., and our three children: Lydia, Tonyé, and Ibinabo, Jr., as well as our son-in-love, Kelcey. These are the people who inspire and motivate me to pursue God the most. I believe I will always have their prayers and support in all my endeavors.

I want to thank the late Billy Joe Daugherty who, along with his wife, Sharon, founded Victory Christian Center in Tulsa, Oklahoma. He and this church inspired me to pursue reading through the Holy Bible. As a result, I have learned to cultivate God's Word, God's presence, and God's faithfulness into my life daily. Because of them, I have become a fan of regular Bible reading and using a plan to help me study its books from Genesis to Revelation. I hope you will try it as well. I believe it will change and improve your life. Doing so will make you unshakable.

Lastly, I want to acknowledge and thank my long-time friend, Dr. Constance Nhira. She is the Vice President of Hope for all Nations

Ministries International in Tulsa, Oklahoma. We have been prayer partners and sisters in Christ since early 1990. She has mentored me with her success in life, marriage, and ministry. Thank you for taking the time to review this Bible study guide and for giving me your heartfelt counsel and honest assessment.

FOREWORD

I have known Merleanna Dick since early 1990. My first experience with her was as a neighbor for two years, which turned into a wonderful friendship. She is a mother of three wonderful children. I was privileged to see them born and grow. She and her husband, Ibinabo Natebo Dick, Sr. became our family friends to this day. After years of praying together, I discovered that Merleanna was a woman of prayer who valued the Word of God to a deeper level. Merleanna has been a chemistry teacher at Oral Roberts University and other schools for several years. She is the Founder and Executive Director of Education for Scholars, and she is passionate about mentoring young people.

Merleanna has written a Bible study guide that is practical, educative, and easy to follow. This book provides great emphasis on the importance of reading the Bible in a year's time. It encourages believers to saturate themselves in the written Word of God and become mature Christians in the LORD. By doing this, one will discover Jesus the manifested generosity of God and become an effective witness and disciple of Jesus Christ. This Bible study guide is a wonderful read for believers, new and old, who desire great intimacy with God. Get ready for the Word of God to ignite your life and change it forever!

Dr. Constance Nhira
Vice President of Hope for All Nations Ministries International
Tulsa, Oklahoma

INTRODUCTION

The purpose of this Bible study guide is to assist you with understanding the organization of the Holy Bible as it relates to the plan of God for humanity. This manual will help you to become effective witnesses to all people – both Jews (people of the Abraham lineage) and Gentiles (all other people groups in the world) – who need to believe in Jesus Christ. In the book of Mark, Jesus commissioned His disciples to proclaim the gospel or good news to everyone. This Bible study guide will help you explore how Jesus Christ has brought salvation to all the people of the world, both Jews and Gentiles. In the scripture below, Jesus visits His disciples after His resurrection and expresses to them what He expected them to do in His earthly absence:

> Later He appeared to the eleven [His disciples] as they sat at the table; and He rebuked their unbelief and hardness of heart because they did not believe those who had seen Him after He had risen. And He said to them, "Go into all the world and preach the gospel to every creature. He who believes and is baptized will be saved, but he who does not believe will be condemned. (Mark 16:14-16, NKJV)

Jesus didn't want His disciples to be fearful but to preach the gospel with boldness. He also does not want you to be timid in your witness of Him to the world. This Bible study guide is a tool to equip you to evangelize to others with the gospel of Jesus Christ. Like that of the early disciples, you will be able to confidently explain that Jesus is the Christ [Messiah], as proclaimed by biblical prophets long ago. You will be able to explain that the Jesus being told about today is the same Person that His disciples spoke and wrote about in the New

Testament (NT). He is a real Person that the prophets predicted to come and recorded about in the Old Testament (OT). Here is an NT passage of scripture that makes reference to Jesus from an OT passage:

> For Moses truly said to the fathers, 'The Lord your God will raise up for you a Prophet like me from your brethren. Him you shall hear in all things, whatever He says to you. And it shall be that every soul who will not hear that Prophet [Jesus] shall be utterly destroyed from among the people.' Yes, and all the prophets, from Samuel and those who follow, as many as have spoken, have also foretold these days. (Acts 3:22-24, NKJV)

Here, the Apostle Peter is quoting Moses from the OT, and he was speaking about Jesus in this passage. Jesus is not only the Man Who walked the earth with His disciples, but He is also in the lives of people worshiping God in churches today. Jesus continues to be proclaimed by believers all over the world. People are believing because the gospel continues to be preached. Jesus' disciples are active in proclaiming Him as the One promised by prophets in the Old Testament and by the Apostles of the New Testament. You can use this manual as a tool to equip you to join others in effectively sharing the gospel. You will be able to give understanding to others that Jesus is the promised Messiah spoken of by Moses and other prophets of the OT, as well as by the Apostles and disciples of Jesus in the NT. This manual will assist you in reading through the Bible, which is important to you connecting the dots of God's redemptive work to restore humanity to Himself.

Why is this manual useful in connecting the OT and NT?

Jesus' birth, ministry, and future return were all foretold by many prophets in the Old Testament (OT) and by Apostles in the New Testament (NT). The NT documents what Jesus declared about Himself, and that which His early Apostles, like Peter, testified. Both the OT and the NT corroborate to make "One Story" about Jesus and the gospel. If you are going to explain to others that Jesus is the Messiah, you need to be able to do it by explaining how these Testaments connect. There are particular passages in the Bible that show that the Jesus you are trusting in for salvation today is the same prophetic Person that was proclaimed in the Old and New Testaments by biblical prophets and Apostles. As a believer, you need to be able to demonstrate – using the scriptures – why you believe what you preach about Jesus Christ. It should be the desire of every Christian to be able to proclaim who the Messiah is to others. By using this manual, you will be strengthened in your belief in Jesus Christ and be equipped to do as you are instructed in 2 Timothy 4:1-5:

> In the presence of God and of Christ Jesus, who will judge the living and the dead, and because he is coming to rule as King, I solemnly urge you to preach the message, to insist upon proclaiming it (whether the time is right or not), to convince, reproach and encourage, as you teach with all patience. The time will come when people will not listen to sound doctrine but will follow their own desires and will collect for themselves more and more teachers who will tell them what they are itching to hear. They will turn away from listening to the truth and give their attention to legends. But you must keep control

of yourself in all circumstances; endure suffering, do the work of a preacher of the Good News, and perform your whole duty as a servant of God. (NLT)

To proclaim the gospel, you must be established in your faith in Christ Jesus. This is especially needed during the difficult times in which we are living. It will be important for believers to know sound doctrine and be able to explain why they believe that Jesus is the Messiah, their Savior, and the Savior of the world (1 John 4:14, ESV).

In the book of Acts, many times, people did not just accept what was preached to them. They studied the Scriptures for themselves. Also, the Apostle Paul and many other New Testament leaders have been known to use the Old Testament scriptures to help people see that Jesus is the Messiah. This practice of studying scriptures is useful for Christians today. There are tools in this manual that will be a great companion for your personal Bible study. Also, the manual can be used as a curriculum in Bible courses to prepare disciples for Christian living and evangelism. Using this manual is helpful in connecting scriptures in the OT with the NT, as you will see in Chapter 3. In that chapter, there are some tables that will assist you in finding passages that are related.

How to use this manual?

At the end of each chapter, there are worksheet pages for students to review scriptures related to the topics covered which will assist in connecting pivotal Bible passages. These scriptures will give you a deeper understanding of the topics covered in each chapter. To help with reading through the Bible by the completion of the manual, each chapter includes a Bible Reading Plan. You may select to use an online Bible plan, like biblegateway.com or my.bible.com to guide you through studying the Bible. Again, this Bible study guide, Jesus the Manifested Generosity of God, is designed with a Bible Reading Plan embedded. Following it or any other Bible plan will help you in your quest to discover that Jesus is the generous gift of God to all of humanity.

The plans and the worksheet pages can be done as an individual study or with discussion groups. You may want to use the scriptural passages for memorization exercises. Individuals or course instructors are strongly encouraged to have the Bible (the translation does not matter) as the main text. At the end of each chapter, there will be scriptures for you to review and a list of terms or concepts for you to research and define. These exercises will help you meditate or ponder scriptures and to clarify the meaning of certain terms or concepts related to each theme covered in each chapter.

CHAPTER 1

Jesus the Manifested Generosity of God

"In this the love of God was manifested toward us, that God has sent His only begotten Son into the world, that we might live through Him" (1 John 4:9, NKJV)

Jesus Christ is the manifested generosity of God to all human beings on the face of the earth. It was God's goodness to give the world His Son [Jesus] to die for the sins of everyone in the world (Romans 3:23-26, NKJV). To give your child to die for someone else is unthinkable, but that was what God sent His Son into the world to do. The promise of this unthinkable act is documented in both the Old and New Testaments. The coming of Jesus was foretold by prophets in the Old Testament. God's plan was uncovered to a man named Abraham who was going to have an offspring that would be a blessing to every person of every race and nation in the world (Genesis 12:1-3, NKJV). Then in the New Testament, it was revealed to us by John the Baptist that Jesus was sent to be the Messiah or Christ, who was to take away the sins of the world (John 1:29 & 36, NKJV). You must make the connection between Abraham and Jesus to appreciate and understand this generous gift of salvation that God provided in Jesus Christ.

Why is this gift God's generosity? Why is the Messiah Important?

This chapter's leading scripture, 1 John 4:9, declares that we have life through Jesus Christ. You may be thinking, "Everybody has life." Yes, everyone has physical life, but not everyone has spiritual life with God. Faith in Jesus Christ gives life that fills your physical life with the abiding presence of God (John 15:5-8, NKJV). God sent His Son, Jesus, into the world to abide within us through His Holy Spirit. This gift of God's generosity is explained in this scripture, "In this, the love of God was manifested toward us, that God has sent His only begotten Son into the world, that we might live through Him" (1 John 4:9, KJV). To give a supporting answer to the questions or an explanation of the need for spiritual life, you must understand God's plan, the life of Jesus, and the purpose of His ministry on Earth. An in-depth study of His life will show how spiritual life is far more than just being alive. As we examine the life of Jesus, we will understand the mystery behind God's generosity and His plan in giving His Son to save or redeem humanity.

God's Plan

Jesus is the human embodiment of God sent to the earth. God came to Earth as a human, in the anointed Man, Jesus Christ. This is the way God planned to redeem us after the fall of humanity with Adam and Eve. The description of Him coming as the Messiah or Christ is presented in Colossians 2:9 and 10 (HCSB), "For the entire fullness of God's nature dwells bodily in Christ, and you have been filled by Him, who is the head over every ruler and authority." God placed Himself in Jesus Christ (the Anointed One). God was in Christ (the Anointed One) doing the work of enabling humanity to be reunited or redeemed to Himself. "…that is, that God was in Christ reconciling the world to Himself, not imputing their trespasses to them, and has committed to us the word of reconciliation" (2 Corinthians 5:19, NKJV). By God becoming a human being in Jesus, He is fully God and fully man. His earthly name is Jesus. His identity of Messiah or Christ is the representation of His assignment to redeem humanity. Jesus is the only anointed human who is holy and righteous enough to redeem humanity. Colossians 2:9-10 (NKJV) demonstrates how Jesus Christ is God's generosity because it shows Jesus giving the totality of Himself to redeem humanity. Jesus has God's nature within Himself, and He gives His nature to those who believe in Him so that He can abide in them. To make this possible, Jesus had to die or give up His earthly body on behalf of humanity. This explains why many commemorate the life, crucifixion, and resurrection of Jesus during what is called Easter. For God's plan to work, there had to be an anointed human substitute for humanity. This was accomplished through Jesus Christ.

You may be thinking someone is generous when they go beyond what is expected or they give more than what is required. God, in Jesus, became God in human flesh and left the amenities of Heaven to come live in the substandard conditions of Earth. However, in this, God is doing more than, for example, Bill Gates leaving his Wellington Estate in Florida to live in the ghetto of New York City. God, in His act of generosity, not only left His throne to live in a human body, but His body was also crucified for us so that we could escape the corruption that leads to eternal death. God was doing more than giving up the comforts of Heaven. He was giving Himself in the Person of His Son, Jesus Christ, to die on our behalf so that we could experience the goodness of His heavenly Kingdom on Earth.

The Life and Ministry of Jesus

While Jesus was on the earth, He taught and demonstrated God's Kingdom to humanity. That is what He spent much of His time doing (John 14:9, NKJV). However, He didn't just teach His Father's ways. His life ended in crucifixion on behalf of the whole world. That is not just a kind gesture of someone going beyond, but it was a personal sacrifice of one's life on the behalf of you, me, and everybody. To top off or cap His generosity, God enables us to have a godly life when we believe in Jesus Christ and what He has done for us. The writer of 2 Peter 1:1-4 puts it in this perspective:

> Simon Peter, a servant, and apostle of Jesus Christ, to those who through the righteousness of our God and Savior Jesus Christ have received a faith as precious as ours: Grace and peace be yours in abundance through the knowledge of God and of Jesus our Lord. His divine power has given us everything we need for a godly life through our knowledge of him who called us by his own glory and goodness. Through these he has given us his very great and precious promises, so that through them you may participate in the divine nature, having escaped the corruption in the world caused by evil desires. (NIV)

God sending His Son and His Son giving His life is the ultimate manifestation of God's generosity. It is important for Jesus to be given so that God could make His plan to redeem humanity a reality. No other human being could qualify to redeem us. Jesus was the only human being Who was also God. However, God wanted to have more than just His presence on the earth. Through Jesus, He could create other sons and daughters with His divine nature. To do that, He needed to become human without losing His divinity because not just any human being could make this type of sacrifice to redeem mankind – the sacrifice needed to be pure and holy like Himself. God coming in human flesh is what was required and the only way. God, in anointed flesh (Messiah or Christ), became a substitute for us through the greatest sacrifice of dying on a cross for our sin. "For He made Him who knew no sin to be sin for us, that we might become the righteousness of God in Him" (2 Corinthians 5:21, NKJV). This was the epitome of Jesus' ministry and ultimately, the purpose of His life on Earth.

What was Jesus' Ministry on Earth?

Jesus was 30 years old when He was baptized by John, His cousin, who was a prophet of God. It is recorded that this was when Jesus started His ministry. His life and ministry were all about bringing life – both physical health and spiritual wholeness.

> When all the people were baptized, it came to pass that Jesus also was baptized; and while He prayed, the heaven was opened. And the Holy Spirit descended in bodily form like a dove upon Him, and a voice came from heaven which said, "You are My beloved Son; in You I am well pleased." Now Jesus Himself began His ministry at about thirty years of age, being (as was supposed) the son of Joseph, the son of Heli" (Luke 3:21-23, NKJV)

Compared to the lifespan of most humans, Jesus lived a short life and was crucified not too long after He was baptized. The Apostle Paul recorded in Romans 1:2-4 that Jesus Christ was human and God.

> The Good News was promised long ago by God through his prophets, as written in the Holy Scriptures. It is about his Son, our Lord Jesus Christ: as to his humanity, he was born a descendant of David; as to his divine holiness, he was shown with great power to be the Son of God by being raised from death. (GNT)

God came to Earth – in Jesus (the Son of God) – as the Messiah or Christ, to redeem humanity. Jesus, in His earthly ministry, displayed God's image in power with many signs and miracles. The scribes, or those that studied and taught the Old Testament, still found the idea that Jesus was the Messiah difficult to believe. The main problem that the early Apostles and believers of Jesus Christ had with the Jews and these Jewish leaders during the days after Jesus' resurrection, was convincing them that Jesus was the Messiah promised by the prophets of the Old Testament.

Like the scribes, the Apostles like Peter and Paul were educated or had to become well versed in the OT, and they were able to use Scriptures to convince many to believe in their Jesus. However, in the book of the Acts of the Apostles, it shows the difficult assignment Apostles and believers of Jesus Christ had in convincing the Jewish people to believe that Jesus was the Messiah. The book provides many accounts of Apostles and believers being imprisoned and beaten for trying to teach Jesus to be the Messiah. Although the Jewish leaders expected the Messiah to come, they did not believe that the Jesus that the Apostles preached was the same Person they were looking for as foretold by OT prophets. Peter, Paul, and the other NT teachers connected passages from the OT to help them illustrate that their Jesus is the same Messiah promised and written about by prophets in the OT.

In like manner, we need to be aware of the OT scriptures that specifically show the relationship of the Jesus that we have received to the One promised in the OT Scriptures. To learn about Jesus as the Messiah in both NT and OT Scriptures, we must start from the book of Genesis, the first book of the OT, and read until we reach the book of Revelation, the last book of the NT. Most people believe that God created everything (Genesis 1:1). But to understand how Jesus is the Messiah or Christ, you need to plan to study all the books of the Bible because they each link to the Apostles and our Jesus. Without being a committed student of the Holy Bible's scriptures, your understanding of how Jesus is the Son of God and the Messiah will be difficult to explain. Also, unlike the unbelieving scribes, we need to believe what we read and allow the Holy Spirit to penetrate our hearts.

The history of Jesus as the Messiah is woven into the stories and prophecies of the OT in the Holy Bible. In addition, certain passages need to be carefully and systematically examined so that Jesus can be revealed to us as the Messiah. Throughout this study manual, certain scriptures have been emphasized to help you understand why God so generously gave Jesus to redeem humanity. When engaging in a thorough scriptural inspection of the Bible, you will see that Jesus as the Christ or Messiah is well represented throughout the Bible. The Apostle Paul, in instructing Timothy, ensured that Scripture is reliable in obtaining truth, "All Scripture is inspired by God and is profitable for teaching, for rebuking, for correcting, for training in righteousness, so that the man of God may be complete, equipped for every good work" (2 Timothy 3:16-17, HCSB). The Apostle Peter joins him by saying, "First of all, you should know this: No prophecy of Scripture comes from one's own interpretation because no prophecy ever came by the will of man; instead, men spoke from God as they were moved by the Holy Spirit" (2 Peter 1:20-21, HCSB).

The Apostles believed Jesus to be the Messiah – or Christ – and the Son of God. They held to this even under severe persecution. They declared that Jesus was incarnate – Who came as God in the flesh to be the redeemer of humanity. This was foretold by the Prophets and the Apostles (Ephesians 2:11-20). Jesus, the incarnate God, had no hesitation in teaching His critics to study the Scriptures because by doing so, they would discover that He is the Messiah. Part of His mission on Earth was to encourage people to study the Scriptures.

> His teaching does not live in you because you don't believe in the One that the Father sent. You carefully study the Scriptures because you think that they give you eternal life. Those are the same Scriptures that tell about me! But you refuse to come to me to have that life. (John 5:38-40, ICB)

1 John 4:9 was mentioned earlier in this chapter. It was indicated in this passage that God came to Earth to give us spiritual life through Jesus Christ. Therefore, we can see that God is good to humanity in two ways. As we study the Scriptures from Genesis to Revelation, it is revealed that God provided a world to nurture those created in His image. Before making mankind, He placed everything

His human creation needed to not only survive but to thrive (Genesis 1:1-27). Secondly, He was generous to redeem humanity after the fall of Adam and Eve. God became a human, in Jesus, to redeem humanity. He not only left His home in heaven, but He also submitted Himself to persecution and a horrifying death to do so. Not only is it generous to give yourself to die, but God in Christ was full of mercy and grace as He did it.

To understand how God acted in generosity, we must see, through the Scriptures, that Jesus, who lived on Earth for 33 years, is the same God of Genesis that created the world. Let's consider this passage found in St. John 1:1-3:

> In the beginning, was the Word, and the Word was with God, and the Word was God. The same was in the beginning with God. All things were made by Him; and without Him was not anything that was made. (KJV)

The Apostle John writes about the Word being Jesus Christ. He became flesh and is called the Word. The same Word that created the world is the same One Who became flesh and died to save the world. So, you see, God's generosity is seen in creation and in the salvation of a soul from sin.

Jesus is called the Word

The writer of the Book of St. John identifies the Word to be God. The question is why is the Word emphasized as God? How do we know that the "Word" the writer is referring to is Jesus Christ? First, John goes on to say in John 1:14, "And the Word was made flesh, and dwelt among us, (and we beheld his glory, the glory as of the only begotten of the Father,) full of grace and truth" (KJV). According to the Free Dictionary by Farlex, Word, in the NT passage of John, is translated from logos (the divine word of God), which is a connotation that the Word (or God) "speaks" and "manifests" Himself through things He produces in the earth by speaking them into existence. Logos derives from "legein" meaning "to speak" (https://encyclopedia.thefreedictionary.com/logos).

In Genesis 1:1-3, the scripture proclaims that God created the heavens and the earth by speaking them into existence. Words are used to speak things, and God used words to pronounce things into existence. In John 1:14, the writer is indicating that God, the Word, became human flesh. The one speaking in Genesis became human. He was called the Word – denoting or signifying that Jesus Christ was in the beginning with God and was God creating the heavens and the earth. God was speaking (logos) through John, the New Testament writer, that by the Word, He is being manifested in the flesh or that God in Jesus Christ is incarnate (flesh). In St. John 15-17 in the KJV, Jesus teaches that He is one with God. But for now, let's look at this passage in St. John 1:10-13:

> The Word was in the world, and though God made the world through him, yet the world did not recognize him. He came to his own country, but his own people did not receive him. Some, however, did receive him and believed in him; so he gave them the right to become God's children. They did not become God's children by natural means, that is, by being born as the children of a human father; God himself was their Father. (GNT)

So then, how did God, the Word, come into the world? It was in the Person of Jesus Christ. This concept made the Jewish leaders infuriated to think someone would make themselves equal to God. Why should we believe that Jesus Christ is God? Why is it important to believe this idea? John is saying that Jesus was the Word – that God was made flesh so that He could become a human to live on Earth. Through Jesus, God was able to come to Earth to sacrifice Himself on behalf of humanity. As you read through the Bible, you will discover how to answer questions like these and get the revelation that Jesus Christ is God in the flesh – that John was writing about Jesus Christ when He was referring to the Word that was made flesh. With an intense study of the Bible and an understanding of how certain scriptures connect, the truth unfolds. Your adventure has just begun.

At the end of this study manual, in Additional Resources, there is information on how to find a monthly Bible reading plan. Regardless of what day of the month you start using this manual, by the end of it, all 66 books of the Bible will be read, and you should have studied them carefully as well. It is a self-paced effort with the goal of finishing the reading assignments in each chapter within a month's time. Get started by completing the reading plan and worksheet that goes along with Chapter 1. Then, read each scripture passage and write a short summary to illustrate that you see the connection of each to the concept that Jesus Christ is the Messiah and the manifested generosity of God.

BIBLE READING PLAN AND WORKSHEET

1st Month Bible Reading Assignment:

Instructions: Designate at least one hour daily to prayerfully read the following passages. Make the goal of completing the reading within the next thirty days: Genesis 1-22, Matthew 1-28, Acts 1-3, Job 1-42, Psalms 1-13, and Proverbs 1-6.

Scriptural Review:

Instructions: Read each passage of scripture and write a short summary. Express in your own words your understanding of Jesus being the manifested goodness of God.

Genesis 12:1-3

_____

_____

_____

_____

Genesis 18:18

_____

_____

_____

_____

Galatians 3:3-9

Acts 3:25

St. John 1:14

St. John 15-17

Terminology Research

Instructions: Research and define each term. You may use a Bible dictionary or concordance and write a short summary.

Holy Spirit

_____
_____
_____
_____

Gentiles

_____
_____
_____
_____

Jews or Jewish

_____
_____
_____
_____

Gospel

_____
_____
_____
_____

Evangelize/Evangelism

_____
_____
_____
_____

Disciples

_____
_____
_____
_____

Christ or the Messiah

_____
_____
_____
_____

Old Testament

New Testament

Worship

Sound Doctrine

Baptism/Baptized

_____

_____

_____

_____

Incarnate

_____

_____

_____

_____

Notes:

_____

_____

_____

_____

_____

_____

_____

_____

_____

CHAPTER 2

Bible Prophecy and the Messiah

"Long ago God spoke to the fathers by the prophets at different times and in different ways. In these last days, He has spoken to us by His Son. God has appointed Him heir of all things and made the universe through Him." (Hebrews 1:1 & 2, HCSB)

What does being the Messiah mean?

God was gracious in letting us know ahead of time in the OT that Jesus would come as the Messiah. God appointed Jesus to be His Son and to be the Anointed One to reunite humanity with Himself. The best way to trace Jesus to be God and the Messiah or Christ from the Bible, is to parallel scriptures that prophesied about Jesus in the Old Testament to those in the New Testament. In this chapter of the manual, we will focus on how Bible prophecy is used to prepare the world for Jesus, the Messiah (the Hebrew word for "Anointed One"), and Christ (the Greek word for "anointed"). Jesus is anointed by God to be the Savior of the world.

First, what is prophecy? Then, why Biblical prophecy? Since this study guide is focused on helping you understand how to present Jesus as the Messiah, before moving ahead to explore the relationship between Bible prophecy and Jesus, let's answer these questions.

What is prophecy and how do we recognize it in the Bible?

To know something before it happens can be a comfort to many people – especially if they are dissatisfied with what they are currently experiencing. God didn't like what was happening to humanity on Earth. After being separated from them, He longed for a reunion and had planned for it. Knowing that Adam and Eve would be tricked by Satan into severing their relationship with Him, God put in place a plan for their redemption through His Son, Jesus Christ. Your reading assignment of Genesis 3 covered the fall of Adam and Eve. God knew that Adam and Eve would encounter Satan in the Garden, and as a result, would sin or disobey by believing that God was keeping something good from them. As a student of the Bible, you need to connect that in cursing the serpent, God was predicting Satan's doom and man's redemption (Genesis 3:14-15).

Prophecy means a prediction or knowledge of future events. Because God is omniscient, He knows everything. Therefore, through prophecy, He makes known, through the Bible, what He has planned for the world and humanity. Plus, He uses human beings to be prophets (people who hear a message from God to share with others). For example, can you recognize this as a prophecy that was given to the writer of Genesis 3:13-15?

> And the Lord God said unto the woman, what is this that thou hast done? And the woman said, the serpent beguiled me, and I did eat. And the Lord God said unto the serpent, Because thou hast done this, thou art cursed above all cattle, and above every beast of the field; upon thy belly shalt thou go, and dust shalt thou eat all the days of thy life: And I will put enmity between

thee and the woman, and between thy seed and her seed; it shall bruise thy head, and thou shalt bruise his heel. (KJV)

The prophecy that God gives the writer in this passage of scripture indicates that the seed of Eve would be an enemy of the seed of the serpent. The seed of the woman, Eve, is the promised Messiah or "Anointed One," and the seed of the serpent, Satan, is the one who put the "Anointed One" – or Jesus to death on a cross later in history. The Messiah is resurrected to heaven, and the seed of the serpent will be cast for eternity into hell. Read Genesis 3:13-15 and Revelations 12:17, 20:1-3, and 19:20 in your Bible, and write a reflection of them in the Scriptural Review section of this chapter. As you read and study the Bible, you must learn to recognize prophetic passages. There are clues in the Scriptures that will enable you to detect when and who God is using to reveal His plan. Sometimes, it might be obvious when prophets write that God said it to them. This is an obvious indicator. However, many times, the writer or writing is not as clear. This passage in Genesis 3:13-15, is a prime example. As you read through the Bible, you will learn to recognize clues that a prophetic message is being provided by God to help us understand His plan for the redemption of humanity.

There is a prophetic theme or thread running through the Bible which says that God created humanity in His image with the sole purpose of having a relationship with them. Statements throughout the Old and New Testaments are arranged strategically by God so that the prophetic messages of the thread can be connected to His redemptive plan or pursuit of being reunited with those created in His image. For the statement of Genesis 3:13-15 to be linked to God's redemptive plan, its interpretation or meaning must be coupled with other passages or statements made by other prophets. In these verses, God was revealing that Jesus Christ was going to be crucified by Pilate (Matthew 27). Genesis talks about the seed of the woman and the seed of the serpent. Matthew speaks of Jesus Christ and Pilate. That is how prophecy works, and it can seem mysterious. Jesus was once asked by His disciples why He taught in parables. He replied, "Because the secrets of the kingdom of heaven have been given for you to know, but it has not been given to them" (Matthew 13:11, HCSB). Perhaps, God gives prophecy for the same reason that Jesus taught in parables. His mysteries are for those of His kingdom or His seed and not for those of the kingdom of Satan and his children. Besides, Satan, the serpent in Genesis, is God's enemy. For strategic reasons, battle plans are kept secret from the opponent. Those of the Kingdom of God have the Holy Spirit to help them understand His secret plan. As you study the Bible, ask the Holy Spirit to help you recognize prophetic passages.

How does Bible prophecy connect Jesus as the Messiah?

A record of God talking about a Messiah to redeem or restore His relationship with humanity is noted in Genesis 3. How does God use this Bible prophecy to reveal that Jesus is the Messiah? The statements made by Biblical writers and prophets and their clues thread or weave together key passages from Genesis to Revelation into the redemptive story of Jesus Christ. This chapter's scriptural reference is Hebrews 1:1 & 2. The writer of Hebrews is explaining that God spoke through prophets, but He is now speaking through His Son, Jesus Christ.

In Matthew 1:18, Jesus is identified as the Messiah, but He is also recorded to be the son of Abraham. In Luke 3:22-38, He is recorded to be the son of David. In other Bible passages, Jesus is called the Son of God. Below are some scriptural passages that give this title or identity to Jesus Christ:

- 1 John 5:20 King James Version

    And we know that the Son of God [has] come, and hath given us an understanding, that we may know him that is true, and we are in him that is true, even in his Son Jesus Christ. This is the true God and eternal life.

- Luke 1:35 King James Version

    And the angel answered and said unto her, The Holy Ghost shall come upon thee, and the power of the Highest shall overshadow thee: therefore also that holy thing which shall be born of thee shall be called the Son of God.

- Mark 1:1 & 2 King James Version

    The beginning of the gospel of Jesus Christ, the Son of God; As it is written in the prophets, Behold, I send my messenger before thy face, which shall prepare thy way before thee.

Mark writes that Jesus is called the Son of God, and He is the manifested Person proclaimed by the prophets. In the OT, the purpose of Bible prophecy is for prophets to deliver the message that God will be sending a Messiah. In Genesis 3:15, a proclamation of crucifixion – "He [Satan] will strike your head" – was given to Eve. Furthermore, in Genesis 12:3b, the promise of redemption was given to Abraham: "All the families on earth will be blessed through you."

Later, in the NT – by John, Luke, and Mark – the manifestation of Jesus as God's Messiah can be found in some passages that parallel OT prophetic passages. Your study of the Scriptures will allow you to see that the prophecy of Jesus Christ is woven throughout the contents of the Bible. Through comparing OT and NT prophetic passages, God's generous gift from heaven that redeems and reunites God with humanity will be noted as you read from Genesis to Revelation.

Chapter 3 provides Table 1: Parallel Scriptural Citations of Jesus Christ in the Bible and Table 2 - Biblical Cross-References of Old and New Covenants to help us with making the comparisons. Also, these tables will assist us in understanding how prophetic passages are threaded throughout the Bible.

BIBLE READING PLAN AND WORKSHEET

2nd Month Bible Reading Assignment:

Instructions: Designate at least one hour daily to prayerfully read the following passages. Make the goal of completing the reading within the next thirty days:
Genesis 23-50, Exodus 1-28, Mark 1-3, Acts 4-28, Psalms 14-23, and Proverbs 7-11.

Scriptural Review:

Instructions: Read each passage of scripture and write a short summary. Express in your own words your understanding that the promise from God to send a Messiah is woven throughout the Scriptures.

Bible Prophecy and the Messiah

Genesis 3:13-15

Revelations 12:17

Revelations 20:1-3

Revelations 19:20

Terminology Research

Instructions: Research and define each term. You may use a Bible dictionary or concordance and write a short summary.

Bible Prophecy

_____
_____
_____
_____

Crucifixion

_____
_____
_____
_____

Satan

_____
_____
_____
_____

Parables

Prophet

Apostle

Notes:

CHAPTER 3

Messiah Paralleled in the OT and NT

"Search the scriptures; for in them ye think ye have eternal life and they are they which testify of me." (John 5:39, KJV)

Parallel Scriptural Citations of Jesus Christ in the Bible

The best way to trace Jesus as God and the Messiah is to study parallel scriptures in the Old Testament (OT) to those in the New Testament (NT). Some believers may be aware that the OT and NT are connected, and that it is one prophetic message about Christ woven within the 66 books of the Bible. This chapter of the manual has two tables. Table 1 provides scriptural citations of the accounts of Jesus Christ in the Old and New Testaments. By comparing these OT & NT Scriptures, the thread of God's plan of redemption for humanity can be followed prophetically.

The Scriptures in Table 1 can seem to be random selections. Often, when the OT prophets gave these proclamations, they would appear to be speaking out of context to what they were saying at the time. This is the nature of how God communicated – or how the prophets probably heard from God. Prophecy is a spiritual experience with God who is Spirit. One NT writer records Jesus as saying, "God is spirit, and his worshipers must worship in the Spirit and in truth" (John 4:24, NIV). Prophets had spiritual encounters with God, and when they would speak, they spoke words from God out of God's Spirit within their spirits. The OT prophets were speaking by God's Spirit about a new plan to send a Person to redeem Israel and all people. They probably didn't fully understand the meaning at the time. The NT prophets and writings were able to connect the prophecies and give meaning to the OT prophetic passages. The writer of Hebrews 9:16-17 reveals that there was a connection between the Old and New Testaments by saying:

> Like a will [testament] that takes effect when someone dies, the new covenant [testament] was put into action at Jesus' death. His death marked the transition from the old plan [testament] to the new one, canceling the old obligations and accompanying sins, and summoning the heirs to receive the eternal inheritance that was promised them. He brought together God and his people in this new way. (MSG)

By paralleling the scriptures in Table 1, you see how prophecies in the OT are fulfilled in the Person of Jesus Christ in the NT. You also see that the manifested generosity of God was prophesied about in the OT and revealed in the Person of Jesus Christ in the NT.

Table 1 - Parallel Scriptural Citations of Jesus Christ in the Bible

Old Testament Citations (prophesied)	New Testament Citations (manifested)
Genesis 3:15 (NIV) And I will put enmity between you and the woman, and **between your offspring and**	Revelation 12:17 (NIV) Then the dragon was enraged at the **woman and went off to wage war against the rest of**

hers; he will crush your head, and you will strike his heel."	her offspring—those who keep God's commands and hold fast their testimony about Jesus.
Genesis 18:18 (NIV) Abraham will surely become a great and powerful nation, **and all nations on earth will be blessed through him.** Genesis 28:4 (NIV) **May he [God] give you and your descendants the blessing given to Abraham,** so that you may take possession of the land where you now reside as a foreigner, the land God gave to Abraham."	Galatians 3:8-9 (NIV) Scripture foresaw that God would justify the Gentiles by faith, **and announced the gospel in advance to Abraham: "All nations will be blessed through you."** So those who rely on faith are blessed along with Abraham, the man of faith. Galatians 3:14 (NIV) He [God] redeemed us in order **that the blessing given to Abraham might come to the Gentiles through Christ Jesus,** so that by faith we might receive the promise of the Spirit.
Deuteronomy 18:15 (NIV) The Lord your **God will raise up for you a prophet like me** from among you, from your fellow Israelites. You must listen to him.	Acts 3:22 (NIV) For Moses said, **'The Lord your God will raise up for you a prophet like me** from among your own people; you must listen to everything he tells you.

Note: This is Moses speaking about the coming Messiah.	Acts 7:37 (NIV) "This is the Moses who told the Israelites, '**God will raise up for you a prophet like me** from your own people." **Note: This is the Apostle Peter speaking about Jesus.**
Exodus 12:46 (NIV) "It must be eaten inside the house; take none of the meat outside the house. **Do not break any of the bones.**" Note: sacrifices were not to have broken bones. **(sacrifices were necessary for sin)** Numbers 9:12 (NIV) They must not leave any of it till morning or **break any of its bones.** When they celebrate the Passover, they must follow all the regulations. Psalm 34:20 (NIV) **he protects all his bones, not one of them will be broken.**	John 19:36 (NIV) These things happened so that the scripture would be fulfilled: **"Not one of his bones will be broken,"** **Note: The writer here is talking about Jesus' bones.**

Zechariah 12:10 (NIV) "And I will pour out on the house of David and the inhabitants of Jerusalem a spirit of grace and supplication. **They will look on me, the one they have pierced**, and they will mourn for him as one mourns for an only child, and grieve bitterly for him as one grieves for a firstborn son.	John 19:37 (NIV) and, as another scripture says, **"They will look on the one they have pierced."**
Psalm 22:15 (NIV) **My mouth is dried up like a potsherd, and my tongue sticks to the roof of my mouth; you lay me in the dust of death.** Psalm 69:21(NIV) **They put gall in my food and gave me vinegar for my thirst.**	John 19:28-30 (NIV) Later, knowing that everything had now been finished, and so that Scripture would be fulfilled, **Jesus said, "I am thirsty."** A jar of wine **vinegar was there, so they soaked a sponge in it, put the sponge on a stalk of the hyssop plant, and lifted it to Jesus' lips.** When he had received the drink, Jesus said, "It is finished." With that, he bowed his head and gave up his spirit. (Also, see Matthew 27:34, Mark

	15:23, and Luke 13:26)
Isaiah 61:1 (NIV) **The Spirit of the Sovereign Lord is on me, because the Lord has anointed me to proclaim good news to the poor. He has sent me to bind up the brokenhearted, to proclaim freedom for the captives and release from darkness for the prisoners.** Isaiah 61:1 (KJV) **The Spirit of the Lord God is upon me; because the Lord hath anointed me to preach good tidings unto the meek; he hath sent me to bind up the brokenhearted, to proclaim liberty to the captives, and the opening of the prison to them that are bound.**	Luke 4:18 (NIV) **"The Spirit of the Lord is on me, because he has anointed me to proclaim good news to the poor. He has sent me to proclaim freedom for the prisoners and recovery of sight for the blind, to set the oppressed free,** to proclaim the year of the Lord's favor." Then he rolled up the scroll, gave it back to the attendant and sat down. The eyes of everyone in the synagogue were fastened on him. He began by saying to them, "Today this scripture is fulfilled in your hearing." Luke 4:18-21 (KJV) **The Spirit of the Lord is upon me, because he hath anointed me to preach the gospel to the poor; he hath sent me to heal the brokenhearted,** to preach

	deliverance to the captives, and recovering of sight to the blind, to set at liberty them that are bruised, To preach the acceptable year of the Lord. And he closed the book, and he gave it again to the minister, and sat down. And the eyes of all them that were in the synagogue were fastened on him. And he began to say unto them, This day is this scripture fulfilled in your ears.
Isaiah 7:14 (NIV) **All right then, the Lord himself will give you the sign. Look! The virgin will conceive a child! She will give birth to a son and will call him Immanuel (which means 'God is with us').**	Matthew 1:20-23 (NIV) As he [Joseph] considered this, an angel of the Lord appeared to him in a dream. "Joseph, son of David," the angel said, "do not be afraid to take Mary as your wife. For the child within her was conceived by the Holy Spirit. And she will have a son, and you are to name him Jesus, for he will save his people from their sins." **All of this occurred to fulfill the Lord's message**

	through his prophet: "Look! The virgin will conceive a child! She will give birth to a son, and they will call him Immanuel, which means 'God is with us.'"
Isaiah 53:4-6 (NLT) Yet it was our weaknesses he carried; it was our sorrows that weighed him down. And we thought his troubles were a punishment from God, a punishment for his own sins! But he was pierced for our rebellion, crushed for our sins. **He was beaten so we could be whole. He was whipped so we could be healed.** All of us, like sheep, have strayed away. We have left God's paths to follow our own. Yet the Lord laid on him the sins of us all.	Matthew 8:14-17 (NLT) When Jesus arrived at Peter's house, Peter's mother-in-law was sick in bed with a high fever. But when Jesus touched her hand, the fever left her. Then she got up and prepared a meal for him. That evening many demon-possessed people were brought to Jesus. He cast out the evil spirits with a simple command, and he healed all the sick. **This fulfilled the word of the Lord through the prophet Isaiah, who said, "He took our sicknesses and removed our diseases."**
Hosea 11:1 (NLT) "When Israel was a child, I	Matthew 2:15 (NLT) and they stayed there until

Messiah Paralleled in the OT and NT

loved him, and **I called my son out of Egypt.**	Herod's death. This fulfilled what the Lord had spoken through the prophet: **"I called my Son out of Egypt."**
Jeremiah 31:15 (NLT) Rachel's Sadness Turns to Joy This is what the Lord says: **"A cry is heard in Ramah—deep anguish and bitter weeping. Rachel weeps for her children, refusing to be comforted—for her children are gone."**	Matthew 2:18 (NLT) **"A cry was heard in Ramah—weeping and great mourning. Rachel weeps for her children, refusing to be comforted, for they are dead."**
Psalm 22:6-8 (NLT) But I am a worm and not a man. I am scorned and despised by all! Everyone who sees me mocks me. They sneer and shake their heads, saying, "Is this the one who relies on the Lord? Then let the Lord save him! If the Lord loves him so much, let the Lord rescue him!" **Note: There is not a direct quote from the scriptures in**	Matthew 2:23 (NLT) So the family went and lived in a town called Nazareth. This fulfilled what the prophets had said: **"He will be called a Nazarene."** **Note: Jesus was called a Nazarene because he lived in Nazareth which was considered a scornful and despised place during his day.** John 1:46 (NLT)

47

the Old Testament where a prophet refers to Jesus as a Nazarene. Deuteronomy 18:15 (NLT) Moses continued, **"The Lord your God will raise up for you a prophet like me from among your fellow Israelites.** You must listen to him.	"Nazareth!" exclaimed Nathanael. "Can anything good come from Nazareth?" John 1:45 (NLT) Philip went to look for Nathanael and told him, **"We have found the very person Moses and the prophets wrote about! His name is Jesus, the son of Joseph from Nazareth."**
Psalm 78:2-3 (NIV) **I will open my mouth with a parable; I will utter hidden things, things from of old— things we have heard and known, things our ancestors have told us.**	Matthew 13:34-35 (NIV) Jesus spoke all these things to the crowd in parables; he did not say anything to them without using a parable. **So was fulfilled what was spoken through the prophet: "I will open my mouth in parables, I will utter things hidden since the creation of the world."**
Isaiah 6:9-10 (NIV) He said, **"Go and tell this people: "'Be ever hearing, but never understanding; be ever seeing, but never perceiving.'**	Matthew 13:14 (NIV) In them is fulfilled the prophecy of Isaiah: **'You will be ever hearing but never understanding; you will be**

Make the heart of this people calloused; make their ears dull and close their eyes. Otherwise they might see with their eyes, hear with their ears, understand with their hearts, and turn and be healed."	ever seeing but never perceiving. For this people's heart has become calloused; they hardly hear with their ears, and they have closed their eyes. Otherwise they might see with their eyes, hear with their ears, understand with their hearts and turn, and I would heal them.'
Zechariah 13:7 NLT "Awake, O sword, against my shepherd, the man who is my partner," says the Lord of Heaven's Armies. **"Strike down the shepherd, and the sheep will be scattered, and I will turn against the lambs.**	Matthew 26:31 NLT On the way, Jesus told them, "Tonight all of **you will desert me. For the Scriptures say, 'God will strike the Shepherd, and the sheep of the flock will be scattered.**
Isaiah 40:3-5 NLT **Listen! It's the voice of someone shouting, "Clear the way through the wilderness for the Lord! Make a straight highway through the wasteland for our**	Luke 3:4-6 NLT Isaiah had spoken of John when he said, "He is a voice shouting in the wilderness, 'Prepare the way for the Lord's coming! Clear the road for him! The valleys

God! Fill in the valleys, and level the mountains and hills. Straighten the curves, and smooth out the rough places. Then the glory of the Lord will be revealed, and all people will see it together. The Lord has spoken!"	will be filled, and the mountains and hills made level. The curves will be straightened, and the rough places made smooth. And then all people will see the salvation sent from God.'"
Psalm 2:6-8 New Living Translation For the Lord declares, "I have placed my chosen king on the throne in Jerusalem, on my holy mountain." The king proclaims the Lord's decree: **"The Lord said to me, 'You are my son. Today I have become your Father.** Only ask, and I will give you the nations as your inheritance, the whole earth as your possession. **Note: David spoke this prophetic word about Jesus Christ.**	Acts 13:32-33 New Living Translation "And now we are here to bring you this Good News. The promise was made to our ancestors, and God has now fulfilled it for us, their descendants, by raising Jesus. This is what the second psalm says about Jesus: **'You are my Son. Today I have become your Father.** Matthew 2:2 New Living Translation "Where is the newborn king of the Jews? We saw his star as it rose, and we have come to

	worship him." **Note: Jesus was recognized as a king of the Israelites.**
Micah 5:2 New Living Translation **But you, O Bethlehem Ephrathah, are only a small village among all the people of Judah. Yet a ruler of Israel, whose origins are in the distant past, will come from you on my behalf.** Note: Prophecy of Jesus' birthplace.	Matthew 2:5-6 New Living Translation "In Bethlehem in Judea," they said, "for this is what the prophet wrote: **'And you, O Bethlehem in the land of Judah, are not least among the ruling cities of Judah, for a ruler will come from you who will be the shepherd for my people Israel.'"**

Biblical Cross-References of Old and New Covenants

In Table 2, there is a biblical cross-reference of scriptures that shows the connection between the promise or covenant God made to Abraham in the OT to the manifestation of that promise in Jesus Christ recorded in the NT. This manuscript includes two blood covenants from the Bible: an old one that started in the OT and was consummated in the NT with a new covenant. Understanding why there are two testaments or covenants (OT and NT) which are one promise being completed in Jesus Christ is important. Both are blood covenants that require blood sacrifices. For many, the thought of a blood covenant can be disturbing. The picture that may come to mind is the cutting of the flesh that two people do to mingle their blood. There is no need for such a covenant between God and humanity for the redemption of humanity from sin. All that was needed was for God to come to Earth in His Son. "For God was in Christ, reconciling the world to himself, no longer counting people's sins against them. And he gave us this wonderful message of reconciliation" (2 Corinthians 5:19, NLT).

As you review the cross-references in Table 2, compare the old and new citations that reveal the connection of the promise made by God to Abraham and his seed in the old covenant to the manifestation of the promise in the new covenant that was accomplished through Jesus Christ.

Table 2 - Biblical Cross-References of Old and New Covenants

Old Testament Covenants (prophesied)	New Testament Covenants (manifested)
Abraham was promised a seed to bless the world.	**Jesus Christ is that promised seed.**
Genesis 12:1-7 (NIV) **The Lord had said to Abram,** "Go from your country, your people and your father's household to the land I will show you. "I will make you into a great nation, and I will bless you; I will make your	Galatians 3:15-18 (NIV) Brothers and sisters, let me take an example from everyday life. Just as no one can set aside or add to a human covenant that has been duly established, so it is in this case. **The promises were**

name great, and you will be a blessing. I will bless those who bless you, and whoever curses you, I will curse **and all peoples on earth will be blessed through you."** So Abram went, as the **Lord had told him**; and Lot went with him. Abram was seventy-five years old when he set out from Harran. He took his wife Sarai, his nephew Lot, all the possessions they had accumulated and the people they had acquired in Harran, and they set out for the land of Canaan, and they arrived there. Abram traveled through the land as far as the site of the great tree of Moreh at Shechem. At that time the Canaanites were in the land. **The Lord appeared to Abram and said, "To your offspring [seed] I will give this land."** So he built an altar there to the Lord, who had appeared to him.

spoken to Abraham and to his seed. Scripture does not say "and to seeds," meaning many people, but "and to your seed," meaning one person, who is Christ. What I mean is this: **The law, introduced 430 years later, does not set aside the covenant previously established by God and thus do away with the promise.** For if the inheritance depends on the law, then it no longer depends on the promise; **but God in his grace gave it to Abraham through a promise.**

The High Priest of Israel sacrificed animals for sin.	**The Blood of Christ replaced animals for sin.**
Leviticus 23:18-19 (KJV) And ye shall offer with the bread seven lambs without blemish of the first year, and one young bullock, and two rams: they shall be for a burnt offering unto the Lord, with their meat offering, and their drink offerings, even an offering made by fire, of sweet savour unto the Lord. **Then ye shall sacrifice one kid of the goats for a sin offering, and two lambs of the first year for a sacrifice of peace offerings.**	Hebrews 9:11-15 (NIV) But when Christ came as high priest of the good things that are now already here, he went through the greater and more perfect tabernacle that is not made with human hands, that is to say, is not a part of this creation. **He did not enter by means of the blood of goats and calves; but he entered the Most Holy Place once for all by his own blood,** thus obtaining eternal redemption. The blood of goats and bulls and the ashes of a heifer sprinkled on those who are ceremonially unclean sanctify them so that they are outwardly clean. **How much more, then, will the blood of Christ, who through the eternal Spirit offered himself unblemished to God, cleanse our consciences**

from acts that lead to death, so that we may serve the living God!** For this reason Christ is the mediator of a new covenant, that those who are called may receive the promised eternal inheritance—now that he has died as a ransom to set them free from the sins committed under the first covenant.

Hebrews 10:4 (NIV)

It is impossible for the blood of bulls and goats to take away sins.

A change in the Old Covenant declared.	The New Covenant is established in Jesus Christ.
Isaiah 11:1-4 (NLT) A Branch from David's Line Out of the stump of David's family will grow a shoot—yes, a new Branch bearing fruit from the old root. **And the Spirit of the Lord will rest on him—the Spirit of wisdom and understanding, the**	Luke 4:18 (NIV) **"The Spirit of the Lord is on me, because he has anointed me to proclaim good news to the poor. He has sent me to proclaim freedom for the prisoners and recovery of sight for the blind, to set the**

Spirit of counsel and might, the Spirit of knowledge and the fear of the Lord. He will delight in obeying the Lord. He will not judge by appearance nor make a decision based on hearsay. He will give justice to the poor and make fair decisions for the exploited. The earth will shake at the force of his word, and one breath from his mouth will destroy the wicked.	**oppressed free, to proclaim the year of the Lord's favor." Then he rolled up the scroll, gave it back to the attendant and sat down. The eyes of everyone in the synagogue were fastened on him. He began by saying to them, "Today this scripture is fulfilled in your hearing."**
David's throne will produce a Savior. Isaiah 11:10 (NLT) **In that day the heir to David's throne will be a banner of salvation to all the world.** The nations will rally to him, and the land where he lives will be a glorious place	Jesus Christ is that Savior. Romans 15:12 (NLT) **And in another place Isaiah said, "The heir to David's throne[a] will come, and he will rule over the Gentiles. They will place their hope on him."**
The Savior will be a fellow Israelite from the lineage of David.	Jesus is of the line of David that the prophets proclaimed.

Deuteronomy 18:15 (NLT) **Moses continued, "The Lord your God will raise up for you a prophet like me from among your fellow Israelites. You must listen to him.**	Acts 3:22 **For Moses said, 'The Lord your God will raise up for you a prophet like me from among your own people; you must listen to everything he tells you.** John 5:46-47 (NLT) **If you really believed Moses, you would believe me, because he wrote about me.** But since you don't believe what he wrote, how will you believe what I say?"
The change in the Old Covenant will still be punishment through blood. Isaiah 53:4-8 (NLT) Yet it was our weaknesses he carried; it was our sorrows that weighed him down. And we thought his troubles were punishment from God, a punishment for his own sins! **But he was pierced for our rebellion, crushed for our sins. He was**	**The New Covenant punishment is by the blood of Jesus Christ.** Acts 8:30-33 (NLT) Philip ran over and heard the man reading from the prophet Isaiah. Philip asked, "Do you understand what you are reading?" The man replied, "How can I, unless someone instructs me?" And he urged Philip to come up into the carriage and sit with him. The passage of Scripture he had been

beaten so we could be whole. He was whipped so we could be healed. All of us, like sheep, have strayed away. We have left God's paths to follow our own. Yet the Lord laid on him the sins of all. He was oppressed and treated harshly, yet he never said a word. He was led like a lamb to the slaughter. And as a sheep is silent before the shearers, he did not open his mouth. Unjustly condemned, he was led away. No one cared that he died without descendants, that his life was cut short in midstream. But he was struck down for the rebellion of my people.	reading was this: "He was led like a sheep to the slaughter. And as a lamb is silent before the shearers, he did not open his mouth. He was humiliated and received no justice. Who can speak of his descendants? For his life was taken from the earth." 2 Corinthians 5:19 (NLT) For God was in Christ, reconciling the world to himself, no longer counting people's sins against them. And he gave us this wonderful message of reconciliation.
Prophecy declares that the Old Covenant will acquire a different sacrifice. Deuteronomy 18:15-19 (NLT) Moses continued, **"The Lord**	Jesus Christ is the different sacrifice in the New Covenant. Acts 3:17-26 (NKJV) "Yet now, brethren, I know that you did it in ignorance, as did

your God will raise up for you a prophet like me from among your fellow Israelites. You must listen to him. For this is what you yourselves requested of the Lord your God when you were assembled at Mount Sinai. You said, 'Don't let us hear the voice of the Lord our God anymore or see this blazing fire, for we will die.' "Then the Lord said to me, 'What they have said is right. I will raise up a prophet like you from among their fellow Israelites. I will put my words in his mouth, and he will tell the people everything I command him. I will personally deal with anyone who will not listen to the messages the prophet proclaims on my behalf.	also your rulers. **But those things which God foretold by the mouth of all His prophets, that the Christ would suffer, He has thus fulfilled. Repent therefore and be converted, that your sins may be blotted out, so that times of refreshing may come from the presence of the Lord,** and that He may send Jesus Christ, who was preached to you before, whom heaven must receive until the times of restoration of all things, which God has spoken by the mouth of all His holy prophets since the world began. **For Moses truly said to the fathers, 'The Lord your God will raise up for you a Prophet like me from your brethren. Him you shall hear in all things, whatever He says to you. And it shall be that every soul who will not hear that Prophet shall be utterly destroyed from among the**

people.' Yes, and all the prophets, from Samuel and those who follow, as many as have spoken, have also foretold these days. You are sons of the prophets, and of the covenant which God made with our fathers, saying to Abraham, 'And in your seed all the families of the earth shall be blessed.'** To you first, God, having raised up His Servant Jesus, sent Him to bless you, in turning away every one of you from your iniquities."

Acts 10:43 (NKJV)

To Him all the prophets witness that, through His name, whoever believes in Him will receive remission of sins."

Luke 24:27 (NKJV)

And beginning at Moses and all the Prophets, He expounded to them in all the Scriptures the things concerning Himself.

The Old Covenant requires a Messiah or Christ (Anointed One)	The New Covenant provided Jesus Christ.
Daniel 9:25-26 (NLT) Now listen and understand! Seven sets of seven plus sixty-two sets of seven will pass from the time the command is given to rebuild Jerusalem **until a ruler—the Anointed One—comes. Jerusalem will be rebuilt with streets and strong defenses, despite the perilous times.** "After this period of sixty-two sets of seven, **the Anointed One will be killed, appearing to have accomplished nothing, and a ruler will arise whose armies will destroy the city and the Temple.** The end will come with a flood, and war and its miseries are decreed from that time to the very end.	John 4:23-27 (NLT) **But the time is coming—indeed it's here now—when true worshipers will worship the Father in spirit and in truth. The Father is looking for those who will worship him that way.** For God is Spirit, so those who worship him must worship in spirit and in truth." **The woman said, "I know the Messiah is coming—the one who is called Christ. When he comes, he will explain everything to us." Then Jesus told her, "I am the Messiah!"** Just then his disciples came back. They were shocked to find him talking to a woman, but none of them had the nerve to ask, "What do you want with her?" or "Why are you talking to her?"

These two tables are included in this Bible study guide to help you identify scriptures in the NT that connect Jesus Christ to the prophetic passages in the OT. Jesus was promised to come as the Messiah or Christ (Anointed One) by OT prophets, and He was referenced in the NT by those who had put their faith in Him – all making declarations of God's generous gift, Jesus Christ, to all of humanity. It is important for us to understand that Jesus Christ was in the plan of God from the beginning – even before the fall of Adam and Eve. Biblical authors started writing about God's redemptive plan with the stories of Adam, Eve, and Abraham in the book of Genesis. From there the stories about God's redemptive plan continued with the story of Moses leading the Israelites out of Egypt in the book of Exodus. All of humanity is loved by God, and He proves it with the promise that all nations will be blessed by Abraham's seed – Jesus Christ (Genesis 18:18 and Galatians 3:8 & 9). In helping the Israelites escape from slavery in Egypt, He preserves one nation that would deliver His seed (Jesus) to save the world. Jesus Christ is the seed of David: "Has not the Scripture said that the Christ comes from the seed of David and from the town of Bethlehem, where David was?" (John 7:42, NKJV). David is of the lineage of Jacob, who was renamed Israel (1 & 2 Samuel).

BIBLE READING PLAN AND WORKSHEET

3rd Month Bible Reading Assignment:

Instructions: Designate at least one hour daily to prayerfully read the following passages. Make the goal of completing the reading within the next thirty days: Exodus 29-40, Leviticus 1-27, Numbers 1-24, Psalms 24-35, Proverbs 12-17, Mark 4-16, Luke 1-2, and Romans 1-16.

Scriptural Review:

Instructions: Read each passage of scripture and write a short summary. Express in your own words your understanding about the OT and NT being connected.

John 5:39

John 19:28-37

Isaiah 50:4-9, 52:13-53:12

Messiah Paralleled in the OT and NT

_____

_____

Exodus 12:46

_____

_____

_____

_____

Numbers 9:12

_____

_____

_____

_____

Psalm 34:20

_____

_____

_____

_____

Zechariah 12:10

_____

_____

Terminology Research

    Instructions: Research and define each term. You may use a Bible dictionary or concordance and write a short summary.

Biblical Cross-Reference

_____
_____
_____
_____

Covenant

_____
_____
_____
_____

Sovereign

_____
_____
_____
_____

Messiah Paralleled in the OT and NT

Parallel Scriptures

Message of Reconciliation

Notes:

CHAPTER 4

Jesus's Mission on Earth

"In my former book, Theophilus, I wrote about all that Jesus began to do and to teach until the day he was taken up to heaven, after giving instructions through the Holy Spirit to the apostles he had chosen." (Acts 1:1-2, NIV)

Chapter 3 of this study guide presented some parallel scriptures of the OT and NT which provide documentation of Jesus being the promised Messiah or Christ. Jesus was prophesied about in the OT and manifested in the NT. The writer to Theophilus says that he wrote about what Jesus did and said while He was on Earth. Everything recorded about Jesus in the NT is directly related to Him fulfilling what was prophesied about Him in the OT.

Jesus lived for 33 years on Earth which is relatively short for most people in the Bible, and the average lifespan for a human today is about 79 years. Nonetheless, in John 21:25, it is written that so much was written about what Jesus did that the world would have difficulty holding the books: "Jesus did many other things as well. If every one of them were written down, I suppose that even the whole world would not have room for the books that would be written" (NIV).

Much of Jesus' life is recorded in the books known as The Gospels: Matthew, Mark, Luke, and John. In this study guide, there is emphasis given to the work of Christ in fulfilling God's plan to restore humanity. The separation that the sin of Adam and Eve caused at the beginning of the world caused the relationship between God and humanity to be broken. In this chapter, the focus is on how Jesus' coming was redemptive to humanity and that everything He did was geared toward fulfilling God's plan. Jesus' purpose is best understood by 1 Peter 2:22-26:

> He never sinned, nor ever deceived anyone. He did not retaliate when he was insulted, nor threaten revenge when he suffered. He left his case in the hands of God, who always judges fairly. He personally carried our sins in his body on the cross so that we can be dead to sin and live for what is right. By his wounds you are healed. Once you were like sheep who wandered away. But now you have turned to your Shepherd, the Guardian of your souls. (NLT)

There are four primary things that this passage of scripture highlights about what Jesus accomplished during those 3 years of ministry. God, through His generosity, sent Jesus to redeem humanity by providing (1) salvation, (2) righteousness, (3) healing, and (4) fellowship with Himself.

Salvation

Jesus personally carried the sins of humanity, saving them from the penalty of death that was received because of the disobedience of Adam and Eve. It seems unfair and confusing that all humanity should receive judgment because of the actions of two people. Adam and Eve were the first carriers of God's own image on Earth. They became responsible, because of their rebellion, for producing sinful humanity. God's image in them as well as their offspring became distorted in them because of sin. God's image was not clearly seen on the earth again until the day Jesus was born. Jesus never sinned and therefore, became the human candidate to produce offspring with the ability to reflect the image of God again and more clearly through their lives. The Apostle Paul declares that when we believe in Jesus Christ, we become new creations (1 Corinthians 5:17).

In Genesis 1:27 it is recorded, "So God created human beings in his own image. In the image of God, he created them; male and female he created them" (NIV). God is a perfect Being, and He created two perfect beings like Himself. However, sin destroyed that quality of perfection in Adam and Eve when they disobeyed God. Sin is disobedience, which is a rebellion that goes against the character of God. What happened is that sin was created in Adam and Eve when they ate what God had instructed them not to eat, and this gave them a character contrary to that of God. Sin made them imperfect and produced death in them. Like God, they had eternal life, but because of sin, they no longer would live forever.

> The Lord God placed the man in the Garden of Eden to tend and watch over it. But the Lord God warned him, "You may freely eat the fruit of every tree in the garden—except the tree of the knowledge of good and evil. If you eat its fruit, you are sure to die." (Genesis 2:15-17, NLT)

First, God has no sin, and second, He is eternal. Adam and Eve could not retain this characteristic of sinlessness when they ate the forbidden fruit. In addition, they then were unable to do like God and produce perfect offspring. God, being perfect, was able to produce humanity that could have lived forever because He is eternal. He had created a Garden with the intent that Adam and Eve would live eternally and produce sinless children that would live forever. But because of their rebellious action, death came – or they died. That is why God sent Jesus Christ to redeem humanity. Salvation was provided through Him so that humanity could return to spiritually producing offspring with godly characteristics again (1 Corinthians 7:14, NLT). One biblical writer puts it this way in Romans 5:15, "But there is a great difference between Adam's sin and God's gracious gift. For the sin of this one man, Adam, brought death to many. But even greater is God's wonderful grace and his gift of forgiveness to many through this other man, Jesus Christ" (NIV). Jesus came with the perfect character of God to bring the generosity of God back to humanity and give them the ability to produce offspring after the image and character of God – not through natural birth between a man and woman (John 3:6, NLT) – but through spiritual birth through the preaching of the gospel of Jesus Christ the same way the believers did as recorded in the Acts of the Apostles. In John 3:7, Jesus called this being "born again" (NLT). "So don't be surprised when I say, 'You must be born again." Everyone who believes in Jesus Christ can have eternal life (John 3:15, NLT). Salvation is how God restores or redeems the offspring of Adam and Eve to the original intent that He had for them in the beginning in Genesis when they lived in His garden.

Righteousness

Jesus has a perfect character because He is God even though He was living in human flesh (John 1:14, NLT). Through Him, God is with humanity on the earth again. He is Immanuel, God with us (Isaiah

7:14, NLT and Matthew 1:23, NLT). Genesis records that God walked with Adam and Eve in the garden and communicated His desires to them (Genesis 1-3, NLT). This intimacy was not the same after the sin and death of Adam and Eve. Because of them, humanity became separated from God and lost their relationship with Him. They, which had been created to reflect God's righteous image on the earth, instead became sinners and altered God's original plan of humankind being like Him and being sinless. What God intended to last forever was taken away, but God made it right again through Jesus Christ: "For God made Christ, who never sinned, to be the offering for our sin, so that we [humanity] could be made right with God through Christ" (2 Corinthians 5:21, NLT). What sin's distortion made wrong; God made right through Christ. Humanity, through faith in Jesus Christ, becomes righteous – or restored – to God's original intent. The meaning of righteousness can be understood from Romans 3:21-26:

> But now the righteousness of God apart from the law is revealed, being witnessed by the Law and the Prophets, even the righteousness of God, through faith in Jesus Christ, to all and on all who believe. For there is no difference; for all have sinned and fall short of the glory of God, being justified freely by His grace through the redemption that is in Christ Jesus, whom God set forth as a propitiation by His blood, through faith, to demonstrate His righteousness, because in His forbearance God had passed over the sins that were previously committed, to demonstrate at the present time His righteousness, that He might be just and the justifier of the one who has faith in Jesus. (NKJV)

When we put our faith in Jesus Christ, we regain the relationship with God that Adam and Eve lost. Christ's righteousness becomes our righteousness, and we have eternal life. Jesus told Mary, one of His disciples, "Jesus said to her, 'I am the resurrection and the life. He who believes in Me, though he may die, he shall live'" (John 11:25, NKJV).

Healing

One writer of the Gospels, Matthew, made it a point to inform us that Jesus was fulfilling a promise made by the Prophet Isaiah, in that He not only provided salvation (Acts 10:43), but also healing. It is explained in this passage below:

> When Jesus arrived at Peter's house, Peter's mother-in-law was sick in bed with a high fever. But when Jesus touched her hand, the fever left her. Then she got up and prepared a meal for him. That evening many demon-possessed people were brought to Jesus. He cast out the evil spirits with a simple command, and he healed all the sick. This fulfilled the word of the Lord through the prophet Isaiah, who said, "He took our sicknesses and removed our diseases." (Matthew 8:14-17, NLT)

This passage is shown in Table 1 as a parallel to Isaiah 53:4-6 in Chapter 3 of this study guide. God's plan included humanity being restored in all aspects of life: body, soul, and spirit by Jesus healing diseases and casting out evil spirits. Jesus was without sin, "For God made Christ, who never sinned, to be the offering for our sin, so that we could be made right with God through Christ" (2 Corinthians 5:21, NLT). Jesus is God made human with the full image of God. Disease and demons could not function in His presence. Isaiah prophesied that Jesus would take away our sickness and heal us. When our bodies get sick with disease or our souls become vexed, we can trust that God has provided healing for us in Jesus Christ.

Fellowship with God

God created humanity with the ability to have fellowship with Him even while they lived on Earth. Like any parent, God takes pride in humanity, and He wants to experience love from what He created. In return, when humanity expresses a desire to have a relationship with God, it is eagerly reciprocated by God. Here is a great way to describe fellowship. Fellowship has a level of intimacy, and it is more valuable than just having a relationship. God desired a relationship with Adam and Eve and designed a way to fellowship with them in the Garden of Eden. The creation of humanity is a way for God to establish His identity and presence on Earth. As mentioned before, God created them in His image and likeness to enable them to produce offspring with the same identity and image. But before Adam and Eve could produce, they sinned and destroyed the purity of who God created them to be and spoiled their relationship and fellowship with God. Sin mauled their association with God, and they were forced out of the garden where God intended for them to have fellowship with Himself for eternity.

In Jesus Christ, this fellowship has been restored for many. Although, it is not indicated by a physical return to the Garden of Eden. However, it is indicated within the spirit of regenerated humanity as a result of salvation. Through faith in Jesus Christ, we have the opportunity to have a relationship and fellowship with God again. Where sin and death were passed to everyone because of Adam and Eve, relationship and fellowship with God are possible to all who believe through Jesus Christ.

> Therefore remember that you, once Gentiles in the flesh—who are called Uncircumcision by what is called the Circumcision made in the flesh by hands—that at that time you were without Christ, being aliens from the commonwealth of Israel and strangers from the covenants of promise, having no hope and without God in the world. But now in Christ Jesus, you who once were far off have been brought near by the blood of Christ. (Ephesians 2:11-13, NKJV)

It was the blood of Jesus Christ and His death that reversed the death that Adam and Eve caused to come to all humanity. Those that believe in Jesus Christ are regenerated and restored in their relationship and have fellowship with God. The writer of Romans 5:17 puts it this way. "For if by the one man's offense death reigned through the one, much more those who receive abundance of grace and of the gift of righteousness will reign in life through the One, Jesus Christ" (NKJV).

BIBLE READING PLAN AND WORKSHEET

4th Month Bible Reading Assignment:

Instructions: Designate at least one hour daily to prayerfully read the following passages. Make the goal of completing the reading within the next thirty days: Numbers 25-36, Deuteronomy 1-34, Joshua

1-12, Psalms 36-46, Proverbs 18-22, Luke 3-24, and 1 Corinthians 1-8.

Scriptural Review:

Instructions: Read each passage of scripture and write a short summary. Express in your own words your understanding of salvation, righteousness, healing, and fellowship with God provided through Jesus Christ.

Genesis 1:27, 2:15-17

_____

_____

_____

_____

Isaiah 7:14

_____

_____

_____

_____

John 21:25

_____

_____

Isaiah 53:4-6

Matthew 1:23, 8:14-17

Acts 1:1-2, 10:43

Romans 3:21-25, 5:17

1 Corinthians 7:14

2 Corinthians 5:21

Ephesians 2:11-13

1 Peter 2:22-26

Terminology Research

Instructions: Research and define each term. You may use a Bible dictionary or concordance and write a short summary.

Judgment

___

Theophilus

___

Garden of Eden

___

Knowledge of Good and Evil

Notes:

CHAPTER 5

The Messiah and the Church

"Oh, give thanks to the Lord, for He is good! For His mercy endures forever. Oh, give thanks to the God of gods! For His mercy endures forever." (Psalm 136:1-2, NKJV)

Everyone has a story of something that happened in their life that is interesting or maybe precious to them. Nevertheless, there is no individual's life that has impacted the world like Jesus Christ. The life of Jesus as the Messiah – or the Gospel of Jesus Christ – is being proclaimed thousands of years after His death, resurrection, and ascension. It was indicated in John 21:25, that the world doesn't have the room to hold manuscripts of the mighty acts He performed. There is so much known about Jesus that His story will continue to be told forever – for eternity. There is hardly a place in the world that His name is not known. In the Acts of the Apostles, the church leaders – like the Apostle Paul – were willing to face persecution and death to ensure that the gospel of Jesus Christ would spread to Asia and other continents of the world (Acts 1-7). Jesus said that even the gates of hell would not be able to withstand the spreading of the gospel of Jesus Christ by the Church (Matthew 16:18).

The account of the Church (an assembly of God's people) is recorded as far back as when Moses lived, "And Moses brought the people out of the camp to meet with God, and they stood at the foot of the mountain [Mount Sinai]" (Exodus 19:17, NKJV). In fact, the life of Jesus Christ was predicted by Moses at Mount Sinai:

> Moses himself told the people of Israel, 'God will raise up for you a Prophet like me from among your own people.' Moses was with our ancestors, the assembly of God's people in the wilderness, when the angel spoke to him at Mount Sinai. And there Moses received life-giving words to pass on to us. (Acts 7:37-38, NLT)

A study of passages in the OT being parallel to passages in the NT (see Chapter 3 of this manual) shows that the Prophet that Moses was talking about was Jesus the Messiah or Jesus Christ.

All over the world, the Church is recognized as a place where people gather to meet with God. People gather to worship this Jesus Christ whose existence Moses predicted to the people of the wilderness – the nation of Israel. Jesus Christ continues to impact lives through the Church by helping people experience salvation, healing, righteousness, and fellowship with God. The Church is being used by God to help reconcile humanity back to Himself (1 Corinthians 5:19).

When Adam and Eve disobeyed God, they opened the door for many wrong things (like blindness, deafness, hatred, murder, diseases of various kinds, etc.) to happen to all of humanity. It was explained in Chapter 4 of this manual how their sinful nature was passed to all humanity. The reversal of the effects of sins was accomplished by Jesus Christ Who came to show His power to redeem. This passage of scripture gives a prime example of what God sent Jesus Christ to do:

> While Jesus was walking along, he saw a certain man. This man had been blind since he was born. Jesus' disciples asked him,

'Teacher, why was this man blind when he was born? Was it because he himself did something wrong? Or was it because his parents did something wrong?' Jesus answered, 'It was not because either this man or his parents did something wrong. It happened so that God could show his great work in this man. While it is still day, we must continue to work. God has sent me and we must do his work. We must work now because it will be night soon. Then nobody can work. While I am still here in the world, I am the world's light.' (John 9:1-5 EASY)

Jesus states that the blindness was not the result of something wrong done by the man nor his parents. God wanted to show His ability to destroy Satan's work brought about by the original sin of Adam and Eve. Jesus Christ is the light that eliminates the wrong things (in this case blindness) that Satan had brought on this child of humanity. Jesus Christ continues to show His power and His light through the Church (Matthew 5:14-16). The time will come when the Church's dispensation or time will end. Jesus said that when the night comes, God's people will no longer be in the world to work. The Rapture, or the taking away of the Church out of the earth by Jesus Christ, has been predicted (1 Thessalonians 4:13-18).

Pairing the Messiah and the Church together is the essential strategy in God's plan to restore humanity. Bible Gateway shows 111 references to the Church in the King James Version of the New Testament (https://www.biblegateway.com). Further, the prediction of the coming of the Messiah is referred to numerous times in the OT. The Bible emphasizes the importance that God places on the Church in the spreading of the gospel of Jesus Christ and to use it in His efforts to reconcile humanity to Himself. You, as a believer in Jesus Christ, are essential to God's plan. God wants you to be equipped for this work. It is paramount that you read through and study the Scriptures to help you with your assignment in the Church to restore others to God. In 2 Timothy 3:16-17, it says:

> All Scripture is inspired by God and is useful to teach us what is true and to make us realize what is wrong in our lives. It corrects us when we are wrong and teaches us to do what is right. God uses it to prepare and equip his people to do every good work. (NLT)

This study guide has included a Bible Reading Plan to enable you to read through the Scriptures that are inspired by God to teach you how to live the Christian life. As a believer in Jesus Christ, you are a member of the Church with the need to be prepared and equipped to help unbelievers come to God and be restored in relationship and fellowship with Him.

BIBLE READING PLAN AND WORKSHEET

5th Month Bible Reading Assignment:

Instructions: Designate at least one hour daily to prayerfully read the following passages. Make the goal of completing the reading within the next thirty days: Joshua 13-24, Judges 1-2, Ruth 1-4, 1 Samuel 1-27, Psalms 47-59, Proverbs 23-26, John 1-10, 1 Corinthians 9-16, and 2 Corinthians 1-13.

Scripture Review:

Instructions: Read each passage of scripture and write a short summary. Express in your own words your understanding of the relationship between the Messiah and the Church in fulfilling God's plan.

Exodus 19:17

_____

_____

_____

_____

Acts 1-7

_____

_____

_____

_____

Acts 7:37-38

_____

_____

_____

_____

The Messiah and the Church

Matthew 5:14-16

Matthew 16:18

John 9:1-5

1 Thessalonians 4:13-18

1 Corinthians 5:19

_____

_____

_____

_____

Terminology Research

Instructions: Research and define each term. You may use a Bible dictionary or concordance and write a short summary.

The Church

_____

_____

_____

_____

Gospel of Jesus Christ

_____

_____

_____

_____

The Messiah and the Church

Nation of Israel

_____
_____
_____
_____

Gates of Hell

_____
_____
_____
_____

Church's Dispensation

_____
_____
_____
_____

Rapture of the Church

_____
_____
_____
_____

Notes:

CHAPTER 6

Jesus Christ A Prophet Like Moses

"For he [Jesus Christ] must remain in heaven until the final recovery of all things from sin, as prophesied from ancient times. Moses, for instance, said long ago", 'The Lord God will raise up a Prophet among you, who will resemble me! Listen carefully to everything, he tells you.' (Acts 3:21-22, TLB)

This chapter's scripture indicates that Jesus Christ resembles or is like Moses the prophet who led and spoke for God to the people of Israel. But, to understand this, there must be an explanation of the purpose of the life of these two prophets (Moses and Jesus).

Moses

Let's be reminded that God spoke to the Israelites through Moses and many prophets of the Old Testament. The reason was to reveal His plan of restoring humanity back into fellowship with Him through this prophet that Moses was speaking about (Deuteronomy 18:15). In the scripture in Acts, the Apostle Paul is explaining that the prophet that Moses mentioned is Jesus Christ and that everyone is instructed to carefully listen to Him because Jesus was coming to speak to them about God and bring them back to God. The work of Jesus exceeded that of Moses who was only leading the Israelites to a promised land. Jesus, as John the Baptist said, "Look! The Lamb of God who takes away the sin of the world!" (John 1:29, NLT). Moses was used by God to rescue the Israelites, but Jesus' work would include all of humanity.

However, God did more than speak through Moses and Jesus. He also established, through them, His tabernacle (or Church) – a temple for humanity to worship and have fellowship with God. Moses' tabernacle was a portable tent, and the people of God had to build it, tear it down, and rebuild it when they had to move around in the wilderness (Exodus 36:8-39:43 & Exodus 40:34–38). This continued until King David wanted to build a temple in a permanent location (Jerusalem), which was built by his son, King Solomon (1 Kings 6 and 1 Chronicles 22). God would come into the tabernacle or temple to visit and speak with His people (Exodus 40:34) – or, an angel of God would appear in the temple at Jerusalem to communicate a message from God. For example, when the angel of God appeared to Zacharias, a priest serving in the temple, to announce that his wife, Elizabeth, would become pregnant (Luke 1:11-15). This was a design of God to have fellowship and relationship with His people. This is how Moses met with God, and it continued with the priests in the temple built by Solomon.

Jesus

God wanted to restore fellowship with humanity after "The Fall" of humanity. He worked with them to help them find a way. With Jesus Christ, a greater work of restoration was accomplished. This point presented by Bob Deffinbaugh is applicable:

> "Does this mean that this extensive material in the Book of Exodus deals with the tabernacle has no clear-cut application

to us? I think not. God has always had a dwelling place in the midst of His people. It was first in the tabernacle, and later in the Old Testament period, it was in the temple. In the gospels, God dwelt (literally "tabernacled") among His people in the person of His Son, the Lord Jesus Christ. Now, in the church age, God dwells in the church." (Deffinbaugh, 2004)

In other words, God has established His fellowship with humanity through Jesus Christ. The writer of Hebrews 1:1-5 gives a full picture of the ministry of Jesus Christ – not only as a prophet with a mouthpiece for God – but also as a way for people to become the "Dwelling Place" of God. In addition to that, He shows humanity God's glory, and He is the Creator of the world:

In the past, God spoke to our people through the prophets. He spoke to them many times and in many different ways. And now in these last days, God has spoken to us again through his Son. He made the whole world through his Son. And he has chosen his Son to have all things. The Son shows the glory of God. He is a perfect copy of God's nature, and he holds everything together by his powerful command. The Son made people clean from their sins. Then he sat down at the right side of God, the Great One in heaven. The Son became much greater than the angels, and God gave him a name that is much greater than any of their names. God never said this to any of the angels: "You are my Son. Today I have become your Father." God also never said about an angel, "I will be his Father, and he will be my son." (EASY)

Jesus is more to God than any other prophet and the angels He has in His service. Jesus is identified as being God's Son. Also, Jesus is a prophet like Moses, in that He established a dwelling place for God. Moreover, Jesus did what Moses could not do because He has authority and identity beyond that of Moses. Hebrews 1:1-5 explains that Jesus has these traits that were not given to Moses nor angels:

- ❖ Jesus is God's offspring which makes Him Divine (God)
- ❖ Jesus possesses and made all things in the world (Creator)
- ❖ Jesus has God's perfect nature which humanity lost (Holy)
- ❖ Jesus' prophetic words are more powerful than Moses' (Perfect)
- ❖ Jesus gives people salvation from their sins (He is Christ or Messiah)
- ❖ Jesus is sitting next to the Great God of Heaven
- ❖ Jesus is called Son while angels are not

How is Jesus a prophet like Moses and why is that important?

God uses Moses to deliver His people out of slavery in Egypt. This story is recorded in the book of Exodus. Jesus, Christ or Messiah, provides salvation from sins for all people. Both Moses and Jesus are attributed to being called deliverers. Moses was sent to bring the Israelites out of Egypt, but Jesus Christ is God coming to the earth to redeem or restore all of humanity from the death that Adam and Eve brought upon humanity because of their disobedience. The account of this story of redemption or deliverance of all humanity can be traced throughout the Bible. The goal of this study guide is to help you discover this story that ties Moses and Jesus in God's plan to redeem all of humanity. God uses Moses to deliver one nation and preserve them, as He was planning to send Jesus through them. Jesus, the Lamb of God, took away the sin of the world. This was proclaimed by John the Baptist in John 1:29. This is why it is important to connect the purpose of Moses to that of Jesus. Jesus is a prophet like Moses. He also is a man like Moses. However, Jesus had to also be fully God and spotless to redeem sinful men.

In conclusion, the deliverance God brought through Moses resembles the deliverance God provided by Jesus. That is the depth of their likeness as prophets. They both were used by God. However, with Jesus, salvation was not limited to a nation. God's deliverance is for all of humanity, and it is extended to whosoever believes in His Son, Jesus Christ. This truth is referenced in these scriptures about the work of Jesus:

- There is salvation in no one else! God has given no other name under heaven by which we must be saved. (Acts 4:12, NLT)
- For this is how God loved the world: He gave his one and only Son, so that everyone who believes in him will not perish but have eternal life. (John 3:16, NLT)
- Anyone who believes and is baptized will be saved. But anyone who refuses to believe will be condemned. (Mark 16:16, NLT)
- And anyone who believes in God's Son has eternal life. Anyone who doesn't obey the Son will never experience eternal life but remains under God's angry judgment. (John 3:36, NLT)

We don't have to remain under the judgment of God because of the rebellious act of Adam and Eve. Anyone who puts their faith in Jesus Christ can be saved, healed, and delivered from the penalty of death and separation from God.

BIBLE READING PLAN AND WORKSHEET

6th Month Bible Reading Assignment:

Instructions: Designate at least one hour daily to prayerfully read the following passages. Make the goal of completing the reading within the next thirty days: 1 Samuel 28-31, 1 Chronicles 1-39, 2 Samuel 1-24, 1 Kings 1-4, Song of Solomon 1-3, Psalms 60-71, Proverbs 27-31, John 11-21, Galatians 1-6, Ephesians 1-6, Philippians 1-4, and Colossians 1-3.

Scriptural Review:

Instructions: Read each passage of scripture and write a short summary. Express in your own words your understanding of how Jesus is a prophet like Moses and why it is important.

Acts 3:21-23

_____

_____

_____

_____

Exodus 36:8-39:43

Exodus 40:34-38

1 Kings 6

1 Chronicle 22

Luke 1:11-15

_____
_____
_____
_____

Hebrews 1:1-5

_____
_____
_____
_____

Terminology Research

Instructions: Research and define each term. You may use a Bible dictionary or concordance and write a short summary.

Moses

_____
_____
_____
_____

Temple in Jerusalem

Tabernacle of God

Resurrection

Ascension

Eternity

Persecution

Notes:

CHAPTER 7

Priest After the Order of Melchizedek

"And Melchizedek, the king of Salem and a priest of God Most High, brought Abram some bread and wine. Melchizedek blessed Abram with this blessing: 'Blessed be Abram by God Most High, Creator of heaven and earth. And blessed be God Most High who has defeated your enemies for you.' Then Abram gave Melchizedek a tenth of all the goods he had recovered." (Genesis 14:18-20, NLT)

Melchizedek is identified as "the king of Salem and a priest of God Most High." He blesses Abram with a proclamation that he was blessed and would be blessed by God Most High. Melchizedek also blesses God Most High. According to a search in biblegateway.com, Melchizedek only appears twice in the Old Testament of the Bible: Genesis 14:18-20 and again in Psalm 110:4. The Psalm scripture is recited again in Hebrews 5:6, 10, 6:20, and 7:17, 21 in the New Testament. All describe Jesus as a priest after the order of Melchizedek. Hebrews 7 has distinctive points that show the attributes of Jesus as a priest like Melchizedek. These are the points from Hebrews 7 that reveal Jesus as God's generosity to humanity:

1. Jesus is the Son of God (Immanuel or "God with us") and a priest forever who brings justice, righteousness, and peace to all who believe in Him. (verses 2-3)
2. Jesus is the greatest of all priests and He was sent to be the One that would bless all of humanity. (verses 4-7)

3. Jesus is a priest unlike Levitical priests who died, but He, like Melchizedek, lives forever. (verses 8-10)
4. Jesus brought a better way for humanity to serve and please God. The priesthood was changed in order for the law to be fulfilled in our lives when faith is put in Him. (verses 11-14)
5. Jesus connects all humanity through His priesthood, which is perfect and full of hope. (verses 15-19)
6. Jesus' priesthood establishes a new covenant (promise or oath) that will never be broken by God. (verses 20-22)
7. Jesus lives forever, and therefore, His priesthood lasts forever. He is with God in heaven to intercede for humanity. (verses 21-25)
8. Jesus was appointed by God to be the High Priest forever because He is God, and He has no sin(s). He is perfect. Unlike the Levitical priests, He only had to make one sacrifice because He gave Himself for the sins of humanity. He was able to do that because of His divinity and holiness. (verses 26-28)

God used Jesus, His only Son (John 3:16), to bless humanity with salvation. Melchizedek was only sent to bless Abraham, but Jesus (the seed of Abraham as indicated in Galatians 3) was sent to bless everyone in the whole world. Levitical priests were given the assignment to sacrifice animals for the Israelites. However, Jesus was sent to bless everyone in the whole world by being the priest and the sacrifice. As proclaimed in John 1:29, "The next day John saw Jesus coming toward him and said, 'Look! The Lamb of God who takes away the sin of the world!'" (NLT).

Both Melchizedek who gave blessings to Abram and the Levitical priests who sacrificed in the temple are dead. Jesus was crucified, but God raised Him from the dead. Jesus Christ still brings salvation from sins to everyone who believes in Him. He is a High Priest living forever in heaven. This includes you and everyone in the entire world – to experience salvation, all you need to do is what Romans 10:9-10 says. "If you openly declare that Jesus is Lord and believe in your heart that God raised him from the dead, you will be saved. For it is by believing in your heart that you are made right with God, and it is by openly declaring your faith that you are saved" (NLT).

Go over the eight attributes of Jesus Christ listed in this chapter. Establish in your heart that God's generosity has been provided for every person – that Jesus is your High Priest and Lord over your life. Endeavor to share this truth with someone today.

BIBLE READING PLAN AND WORKSHEET

7th Month Bible Reading Assignment:

Instructions: Designate at least one hour daily to prayerfully read the following passages. Make the goal of completing the reading within the next thirty days: 2 Chronicles 1-21, 1 Kings 5-22, 2 Kings 1-8, Song of Solomon 4-8, Ecclesiastes 1-12, Obadiah 1, Psalms 72-83, Proverbs 1-5, Mark 1-16, 1 Thessalonians 1-5, 2 Thessalonians 1-3, 1 Timothy 1-6, and Colossians 4.

Scriptural Review:

Instructions: Read each passage of scripture and write a short summary. Express in your own words why Jesus is a priest after the order of Melchizedek.

Genesis 14:18-20

_____
_____
_____
_____

Psalm 110:4

_____
_____
_____
_____

Hebrews 5:2 & 10

_____
_____
_____
_____

Hebrews 6:10

Hebrews 7:1-3

Hebrews 7:4-7

Hebrews 7:8-10

Hebrews 7:11-14

Hebrews 7:15-19

Hebrews 7:20-22

Hebrews 7:23-25

Hebrews 7:26-28

_____

_____

_____

_____

John 3:16

_____

_____

_____

_____

Terminology Research

Instructions: Research and define each term. You may use a Bible dictionary or concordance and write a short summary.

Melchizedek

_____

_____

_____

_____

Priest After the Order of Melchizedek

Immanuel

___

Levitical Priests

___

Priesthood

___

Intercede

___

Divinity

Holiness

Notes:

Priest After the Order of Melchizedek

CHAPTER 8

The Nation of Israel is Important to Salvation

"For Abraham will certainly become a great and mighty nation, and all the nations of the earth will be blessed through him." (Genesis 18:18, NLT)

The purpose of this study guide is to help you understand why and how Jesus is the Christ or Messiah. Further, it is meant to help you understand how He is the offspring or seed that God uses to redeem us. This study guide was written to help bring clarity about Jesus being the Man chosen to restore us to relationship and fellowship with God in the way humanity had it before Adam and Eve sinned in the Garden of Eden (Genesis 2). It can be used to help you, as a believer in Jesus, to articulate to unbelievers what Jesus did for humanity in His life, death, and resurrection. Most importantly, this tool can help with understanding the connection between the nation of Israel and your salvation.

In this chapter, we will cover how Abraham's lineage is wrapped in the plan of God to manifest His generosity in the one Man, Jesus Christ. Through Abraham, God sets the nation of Israel apart as His special people to use them in His plan to redeem the whole of humanity (Psalm 105:43, NLT). He established a covenant with Israel, through Abraham and his descendants, with the plan to bring humanity back into the relationship and fellowship with God in the way they had it before Adam and Eve sinned.

In Chapter 4 of this study guide, Jesus' Mission on Earth, it is explained how Adam and Eve sinned by disobeying God's instruction.

> The Lord God made all kinds of trees grow out of the ground. Trees that were pleasing to the eye and good for food. In the middle of the garden were the tree of life and the tree of the knowledge of good and evil. And the Lord God commanded the man, 'You are free to eat from any tree in the garden; but you must not eat from the tree of the knowledge of good and evil, for when you eat from it you will certainly die.' (Genesis 2:9, 16-17, NIV)

As a result of their rebellion, humanity was born after the image of Adam's sinful nature and likeness. Sin distorted God's image within them when they died. Being distorted meant that they experienced an alteration of the original form of God's image. This passage of scripture gives an account of what happened to the image of Adam and Eve and their offspring:

> This is the written account of the descendants of Adam. When God created human beings, he made them to be like himself. He created them male and female, and he blessed them and called them "human." When Adam was 130 years old, he became the father of a son who was just like him—in his very image. He named his son Seth. (Genesis 5:1-3, NLT)

When God created humanity, Adam and Eve had the likeness of God. However, when they sinned, they started giving birth to offspring after their fallen and sinful image. God comes to Earth Himself to produce offspring after His kind again. God does this in the person of Jesus, His seed or His Son. The difference is Jesus didn't create offspring through giving natural birth. He produced offspring through the power of the Holy Spirit. He regenerates them, making them born again in their spirits (John 3:16). This is covered in Chapter 9 of this study guide. God's plan is to produce offspring in His image and likeness again through His Son, Jesus the Christ, or Messiah.

Jesus Christ the Son of God and the Seed of Abraham

Jesus identified Himself as being equal with or one with God by making this statement recorded in John 10:30: "The Father and I are one" (NLT). When John was baptizing Jesus, a voice was heard from heaven saying that Jesus was the Son of God.

> Then Jesus went from Galilee to the Jordan River to be baptized by John. But John tried to talk him out of it. "I am the one who needs to be baptized by you," he said, so why are you coming to me?" But Jesus said, "It should be done, for we must carry out all that God requires." So John agreed to baptize him. After his baptism, as Jesus came up out of the water, the heavens were opened and he saw the Spirit of God descending like a dove and settling on him. And a voice from heaven said, "This is my dearly loved Son, who brings me great joy." (Matthew 3:13-17, NLT)

Both of these scriptural accounts point to the fact that Jesus' identity was directly related to God and that He was a fleshly representation of God in the earth – the Son of God. There are passages written by the Prophet Isaiah and in the book of Matthew that declare Immanuel, meaning "God with us" (Isaiah 7:14 and Matthew 1:23). For human offspring to be produced, there must be two human beings – a man and a woman. Adam and Eve were used to start the population of humanity. For God to enable the reproduction of His regenerated offspring, He starts with Abraham and the nation of Israel. He makes a covenant with Abraham – the Father of the nation of Israel – to produce His seed, Jesus (Genesis 12:1-3 and Galatians 3:16). And then from Jesus, a multitude of offspring living in unity with Himself is produced. Those who put their faith in Jesus Christ are regenerated and are restored with the ability to reflect God's image and likeness. God starts His regenerated population by making covenant – or being a husband with a nation. In Isaiah 54:5, the Prophet Isaiah declared that God became a husband to the nation of Israel -- "For your Creator will be your husband; the Lord of Heaven's Armies is his name! He is your Redeemer, the Holy One of Israel, the God of all the earth" (NLT). This scripture presents God as not only a husband, but also as a Redeemer. God, through covenant with Abraham and the nation of Israel produces Christ, the seed of Abraham. According to Galatians, Jesus Christ is the offspring of Abraham. "The promises were spoken to Abraham and to his seed. Scripture does not say 'and to seeds,' meaning many people, but 'and to your seed,' meaning one person, who is Christ" (NIV). God's regenerated population comes through Jesus Christ.

Seed of Abraham and the Nation of Israel

God's journey of restoring humanity after the rebellion of Adam and Eve is initiated with a covenant between Himself and a man called Abram, who was later called Abraham. To find the genealogy of Jesus or the Messiah starting with Abraham, read Matthew 1:1-17. Verse two lists Abraham as being the father of Isaac, and the ancestry includes Jesus being born of Mary as seen in verse 16. It is important to note that Jesus' ancestry includes Abraham because of the promise God made to Abraham that all nations would be blessed through him (Genesis 18:18).

As noted in Chapter 4 of this study guide, "What sin's distortion made wrong, God made right through Christ [the Messiah]. Humanity, through faith in Jesus Christ, becomes righteous – or restored – to God's original intent." God intended for humanity to be like Him and to have His image from the beginning of creation. In the next section of this chapter, there is an explanation of how, as recorded in Matthew 1:1-17, the start of God's plan is with Abraham and ends with Jesus being the Messiah or Christ. Jesus Christ is the One to redeem humanity back to God and to restore humanity to have His image and likeness on Earth again. This was God's plan even before the beginning of the world and the rebellion of Adam and Eve.

God's Promise Fulfilled in Jesus – the Seed of Abraham

A record of God selecting Abraham is found in chapters 12-21 in the book of Genesis. God, through the supernatural, helps Abraham's wife, Sarah, to have a baby although she had reached the age of not being able to conceive a child. Sarah gives birth to a son, Isaac, whose birth is recorded in Genesis 21. Isaac's birth is a result of a promise that God made to Abraham that is first mentioned in Genesis 12:1-3:

> The Lord had said to Abram, "Leave your native country, your relatives, and your father's family, and go to the land that I will show you. I will make you into a great nation. I will bless you

and make you famous, and you will be a blessing to others. I will bless those who bless you and curse those who treat you with contempt. All the families on earth will be blessed through you." (NLT)

Understanding this passage helps you to connect how God initiated a plan for His God-seed (Jesus) to get into the earth as a Man. It helps you to make the connection of what God said to Abraham and what the NT writer is saying about believers in Jesus here:

> For you are all children of God through faith in Christ Jesus. And all who have been united with Christ in baptism have put on Christ, like putting on new clothes. There is no longer Jew or Gentile, slave or free, male and female. For you are all one in Christ Jesus. And now that you belong to Christ, you are the true children of Abraham. You are his heirs, and God's promise to Abraham belongs to you. (Galatians 3:26-29, NLT)

All true offspring of God come through Jesus Christ, the seed of Abraham. Following the journey of Christ to the earth and solving the mystery of salvation involves connecting Abraham to the offspring of Isaac's son, Jacob, who through four women, gives birth to the twelve tribes of the nation of Israel. Abraham had Isaac who had two sons: Jacob and Esau. Matthew 1:2 records that Isaac had Jacob who had Judah and his brothers. Judah was one of the twelve brothers that Jacob's two wives and two concubines gave birth to during the time Jacob lived in Haran (Genesis 27- 33). Jacob's name was changed to Israel as a way of God solidifying that He would keep the original promise made to his ancestor, Abraham. Jacob reminded God of this promise as he prayed:

> Then Jacob prayed, "O God of my father Abraham, God of my father Isaac, Lord, you who said to me, 'Go back to your country and your relatives, and I will make you prosper,' I am unworthy of all the kindness and faithfulness you have shown your servant. I had only my staff when I crossed this Jordan, but now I have become two camps. Save me, I pray, from the hand of my brother Esau, for I am afraid he will come and attack me, and also the mothers with their children. But you have said, 'I will surely make you prosper and will make your descendants like the sand of the sea, which cannot be counted.' (Genesis 32:9-12, NIV)

As Jacob continues to wrestle in prayer with God, he receives a blessing. God changes his name from Jacob to Israel. "Then the man said, "Your name will no longer be Jacob, but Israel because you have struggled with God and with humans and have overcome" (Genesis 32:28, NIV). This is where God affirms with Jacob that He was going to continue completing His promise to Abraham through him and his descendants.

Another step in the journey of understanding how God is fulfilling His promise is connecting the birth of Jesus to God's plan. In Matthew 1:16, there is a second Jacob in the ancestry of Israel. His son, Joseph, is engaged to Mary who gives birth to Jesus. To conceptualize the importance of Israel to the salvation of humanity is to see that Jesus is found in the ancestry or lineage of Abraham. The Bible not only has the genealogy of Jesus in Matthew 1:1-17, but it can also be reviewed in Luke 3:23-38. In both accounts, Abraham is mentioned, and this indicates that God was keeping the original promise that through the seed of Abraham all of humanity would be blessed. One writer puts it this way, "God gave the promises to Abraham and his child. And notice that the Scripture doesn't say 'to his children,' as if it meant many descendants. Rather, it says 'to his child'—and that, of course, means Christ" (Galatians 3:16, NLT). Jesus Christ is the seed of Abraham, and through Him, God generates offspring to be created in His image and likeness without distortion.

To summarize, God has a covenant with Abraham and his seed, Jesus Christ. God's plan includes Israel and all nations of the earth. He intends on having one nation serving Him as one people:

> For Christ, himself has brought peace to us. He united Jews and Gentiles into one people when, in his own body on the cross, he broke down the wall of hostility that separated us. He did this by ending the system of law with its commandments and regulations. He made peace between Jews and Gentiles by creating in himself one new people from the two groups [Jews and Gentiles]. Together as one body, Christ reconciled both groups to God by means of his death on the cross, and our hostility toward each other was put to death. (Ephesians 2:14-16, NLT)

In God's new world of His offspring, there will be one nation or "one people" reflecting His likeness and image without the distortion of sin. All those in Jesus Christ have put off the sinful image of Adam and have taken on the pure image of God again. The supernatural seed of God is Jesus Christ brought to the world as a result of God keeping His promise to Abraham. This seed blesses all nations of the world with the ability to be back in relationship and fellowship with God. Anyone who puts their faith in Jesus Christ will be regenerated (born again) to reflect God's likeness and image without sin distorting it. They are righteous with the pure image of God; a holy nation bringing God praise and glory (1 Peter 2:5).

BIBLE READING PLAN AND WORKSHEET

8th Month Bible Reading Assignment:

Instructions: Designate at least one hour daily to prayerfully read the following passages. Make the goal of completing the reading within the next thirty days: 2 Chronicles 22-28, 2 Kings 9-16, Joel 1-3, Jonah 1-4, Amos 1-9, Isaiah 1-34, Psalms 84-96, Proverbs 6-10, Matthew 1-23, 2 Timothy 1-4, Titus 1-3, and Philemon 1.

Scriptural Review:

Instructions: Read each passage of scripture and write a short summary.

Matthew 1:1-17

_____

_____

_____

_____

Genesis 12:1-3

_____

_____

The Nation of Israel is Important to Salvation

_____
_____

Genesis 18:18

_____
_____
_____
_____

Galatians 3:26-29

_____
_____
_____
_____

Terminology Research

Instructions: Research and define each term. You may use a Bible dictionary or concordance and write a short summary.

Nation of Israel

_____
_____
_____
_____

The Nation of Israel is Important to Salvation

Adam and Eve

_____
_____
_____
_____

Garden of Eden

_____
_____
_____
_____

Sinful Nature

_____
_____
_____
_____

Image of Adam and Eve

_____
_____
_____
_____

The Nation of Israel is Important to Salvation

Image of God

_____
_____
_____
_____

Tree of the Knowledge of Good and Evil

_____
_____
_____
_____

Tree of Life and the Knowledge of Good and Evil

_____
_____
_____
_____

Jesus Christ

_____
_____
_____
_____

Notes:

The Nation of Israel is Important to Salvation

CHAPTER 9

Salvation and the Holy Spirit

"The jailer called for lights and ran to the dungeon and fell down trembling before Paul and Silas. Then he brought them out and asked, 'Sirs, what must I do to be saved?" They replied, "Believe in the Lord Jesus and you will be saved, along with everyone in your household." (Acts 16:29-31, NLT)

Like most people, after the jailer encounters the power of the gospel, he wants to know how to receive salvation. He finds out from Paul and Silas that achieving salvation is not difficult. All that is required is that he and his family believe in the Lord Jesus Christ, and they would be saved. As the scripture declares, "For I am not ashamed of the gospel, because it is the power of God that brings salvation to everyone who believes: first to the Jew, then to the Gentile" (Romans 1:16, NIV). Anyone can receive salvation just by believing in the Lord Jesus Christ.

At the moment of believing, the Holy Spirit changes the sinful nature of a person into a righteous one and the image of God is reflected again through their human spirit. Reflect means to make apparent or manifest. Sin no longer has the power to distort the image of God in a person when they receive salvation. Their human spirit becomes filled with God's Holy Spirit and presence. This is known as becoming a "New Creation in Christ" or being "Born Again". "Therefore, if anyone is in Christ, he is a new creation; old things have passed away; behold, all things have become new" (2 Corinthians 5:17, NKJV). Another Bible translation says it like this, "Whoever is a believer in Christ is a new creation. The old way of living has disappeared. A new way of living has come into existence" (2 Corinthians 5:17, GW). Without being born again, the sinful nature prevents a person from reflecting the image of God that is within them from physical birth. As a new creation, the power of the Holy Spirit within a believer causes them to reflect God's image. This reflection to others makes them become a witness of Jesus Christ, Who is the manifested generosity of God within them.

Salvation is the work of God the Holy Spirit, who is the Person of Jesus Christ on the earth. Before His crucifixion, Jesus told His followers that He was going to send the Holy Spirit to fill them (John 14:15-31). He knew the Holy Spirit would have an essential role in helping people receive salvation as well as empowering them to help others to receive salvation. Jesus told them they would receive power from the Holy Spirit:

> And He [Jesus] said to them, "It is not for you to know times or seasons which the Father has put in His own authority. But you shall receive power when the Holy Spirit has come upon you; and you shall be witnesses to Me in Jerusalem, and in all Judea and Samaria, and to the end of the earth." (Acts 1:7-8, NKJV)

Salvation is the work of the Holy Spirit within a person. It is the job of the Holy Spirit to bring you into salvation through your faith in Jesus Christ. The Holy Spirit is the third personality of the Trinity of God. It can be difficult to understand the oneness of God in the

Trinity. However, the Trinity becomes understandable to you when you get saved because at that moment you experience all three of God's personalities – God the Father, God the Son, and God the Holy Spirit. In salvation, or when you become a new creation, you gain a relationship with God and can fellowship with Him through all His personalities (Father, Son, and Holy Spirit). You learn how to pray to the Father in His Son's [Jesus Christ] name and be empowered by the Holy Spirit to do the works of helping others believe. In Acts 1:8, Jesus told His disciples, "..you will be my witnesses" (NIV). The salvation experience involves the Trinity, and God delivers the process to you through three baptisms.

Three Baptisms

In the Book of Acts, the salvation experience is recorded as being associated with three baptisms: (1) John's Baptism to Repentance, (2) Jesus' Baptism to Salvation, and (3) the Holy Spirit's Baptism of Power. You will be given more details about these baptisms in the next three sections. There is a fourth section on the Trinity – Experience with the Trinity. You can understand the Trinity as a result of your experience of salvation through faith in Jesus Christ. Let's look at how baptism relates to salvation.

John's Baptism to Repentance

Jesus was baptized in water by John the Baptist, who was going about baptizing all the Jewish people who were turning back to God and repenting of their sins (Matthew 3). This baptism is mentioned again in Acts 19:4 where Paul said, "John's baptism was a baptism of repentance. He told the people to believe in the one coming after him, that is, in Jesus" (NIV). This act of repentance was associated with the baptizing in water by a prophet called John. The people (probably Israelites) being baptized were signifying to others that they were turning back to God. This baptism was known as the Baptism of John:

> While Apollos was at Corinth, Paul took the road through the interior and arrived at Ephesus. There he found some disciples and asked them, "Did you receive the Holy Spirit when you believed?" They answered, "No, we have not even heard that there is a Holy Spirit." So Paul asked, "Then what baptism did you receive?" "John's baptism," they replied. (Acts 19:1-3 NIV)

In Matthew 3:11, the Apostle Matthew quotes the Prophet John who said that Jesus was coming to baptize people with the Holy Spirit. "I [John the Baptist] baptize you with water for repentance. But after me comes one who is more powerful than I, whose sandals I am not worthy to carry. He will baptize you with the Holy Spirit and fire" (NIV). John the Baptist's assignment from God was to help people turn to God but he didn't have the power or fire to render salvation nor the Holy Spirit (Matthew 3:1-10). Only Jesus Christ – or Messiah – has the power to save and make people become sanctified (New Creations) or be empowered to live free from sin (Matthew 3:11-17).

Jesus' Baptism to Salvation

John's Baptism focused on people repenting, which means to have a change of mind or to turn around and go in a different direction.

> "John went to many places near the River Jordan and spoke a message from God. 'You have done many wrong things,' he taught everybody. 'You must turn away from them and change how you live. Then God will forgive you and I will baptize you.' (Luke 3:3 EASY)

John's ministry involved people turning away from sin, and then they would be baptized in water. However, he knew that this was just the beginning, and he taught them that the Messiah (or Christ) was coming to give them the power to overcome sin. Eventually, it was revealed that Jesus was the Messiah. When people experience Jesus Christ through the power of the Holy Spirit, they will become born again – a new creation. Becoming a new creation is Jesus' Baptism to Salvation in our lives.

However, people can repent and even be baptized with water (John's Baptism), but not be born again (Jesus' Baptism). This is what Paul was helping the Ephesians to understand (Acts 19:1-3). Others go to church weekly, but they never experience the power of the Holy Spirit in their lives. Many people believe, but they still question their salvation. The Apostle Paul encountered such people in Acts 19:4-6:

> Paul said, "John's baptism was a baptism of repentance. He told the people to believe in the one coming after him, that is, in Jesus." On hearing this information from [Paul], they were baptized in the name of the Lord Jesus. When Paul placed his hands on them, the Holy Spirit came on them, and they spoke in tongues and prophesied. (NIV)

The Apostle Paul helped the people recognize that they had something missing in their lives even after being water baptized. Many like them today, have not experienced this baptism in the name of the Lord Jesus. Jesus' Baptism is the experience of salvation that John the Baptist was talking about with his followers – the experience that would come through the Messiah. Many people believe and probably call themselves Christians. However, do they truly have salvation, and are they born again by the Holy Spirit? They need to turn from sin as John the Baptist taught and have Jesus' Baptism to salvation that comes through the power of the Holy Spirit. This will remove any doubt from their minds and hearts. Being born again involves more than repentance or a change of mind. This salvation experience is a baptism that transforms a person from living the unregenerate way to living the way God intended from the beginning of the world. They become empowered to live the way God intended Adam and Eve to live – being in relationship and fellowship with Him in the Garden. God made them both in the image and likeness of Himself. "So God created man in his own image, in the image of God created [him]; male and female created [them]" (Genesis 1:27, KJV). This salvation experience that comes as a result of accepting Jesus Christ is what the writer in 2 Corinthians 5:17 calls "a new creation" (NKJV).

It is not enough to repent, but you must trust that by believing in Jesus Christ you will be changed from the likeness of Adam or Eve to the likeness of God. God, through your faith in Jesus Christ, uses the Holy Spirit to transfer you from Satan's kingdom to His Kingdom. "For he has rescued us from the kingdom of darkness and transferred us into the Kingdom of his dear Son, who purchased our freedom and forgave our sins" (Colossians 1:13-14, NLT). In the Kingdom of His dear Son, you are a new creation through Jesus' Baptism to Salvation.

Water baptism is an essential step in your decision to turn away from sin. However, being born again happens by God sealing you with His Holy Spirit. "In him you also, when you heard the word of truth, the gospel of your salvation, and believed in him, were sealed with the promised Holy Spirit" (Ephesians 3:13 ESV). This means your spirit is born of God's Holy Spirit, making you a new creation – or causing you to be regenerated in your relationship and fellowship with God.

Holy Spirit's Baptism of Power

Jesus told His disciples when He visited them after His resurrection, "But you will receive power when the Holy Spirit comes on you; and you will be my witnesses in Jerusalem, and in all Judea and Samaria, and to the ends of the earth" (Acts 1:8, NIV). In the account of Paul's meeting with the Ephesians in Acts 19, people spoke in tongues and prophesied. They experienced power or the ability to speak in unknown tongues – to speak supernaturally in languages they had not learned or been taught. This was the same experience believers had when they first encountered the Holy Spirit's baptism of power in Acts 2. However, another significant thing that Jesus told His disciples is that they would have the power to be a witness. After receiving Jesus' Baptism to Salvation, you become a powerful witness at home and all over the world. The ultimate sign of the baptism of the Holy Spirit in a believer is the believer having the ability to reproduce themselves – the Jesus lifestyle they have – in the lives of others. Remember what was covered in Chapter 4 of this study manual. Jesus' mission on Earth was to restore humanity back to God. It was not only for humanity to repent or return in a mental sense, but it was for humanity to be regenerated (renewed or restored). It was for them to turn from Adam's image and likeness to being able to reflect God's image and likeness in their lives. The salvation experience is for you to be regenerated (renewed or restored) back to God's presence and power. The salvation experience is for you to have the ability, through the power of the Holy Spirit, to be like His original creation that was lost as a result of Adam's disobedience in the Garden of Eden.

The tongues and the prophesying that believers exhibited in Acts 2 and Acts 19 are signs of the Holy Spirit's work of salvation taking place in their lives. But most importantly, believers received the power to help others be regenerated back to reflecting God's image. This study guide covers how God uses Jesus Christ to reproduce offspring that have the power to reflect His image to others in the world. The Holy Spirit in you has all the gifts you need to enable you to fulfill God's plan of equipping you to be Jesus' witnesses. To learn about the gifts of the Holy Spirit, read I Corinthians 12-14. You will discover that there are more gifts than tongues and prophesying. However, the ultimate purpose for the power of the Holy Spirit's baptism and these gifts is to make you a witness to bring people back to God.

Experience with the Trinity

With Jesus' Baptism to Salvation and the Holy Spirit's Baptism of Power, you receive a revelation of The Trinity – the three personalities of God: Father, Son, and Holy Spirit. Something that has been confusing before salvation is now understood by your encounter with God through the Holy Spirit. Your spirit is united to God's Spirit. This experience with the Holy Spirit is explained in Romans 8:12-17:

> Therefore, dear brothers and sisters, you have no obligation to do what your sinful nature urges you to do. For if you live by its dictates, you will die. But if through the power of the Spirit you put to death the deeds of your sinful nature, you will live. All who are led by the Spirit of God are children of God. So you have not received a spirit that makes you fearful slaves. Instead, you received God's Spirit when he adopted you as his own children. Now we call him, "Abba, Father." For his Spirit joins with our spirit to affirm that we are God's children. And since we are his children, we are his heirs. In fact, together with Christ we are heirs of God's glory. But if we are to share his glory, we must also share his suffering. (NLT)

Through Jesus' Baptism to Salvation, you gain experience with God as "Abba, Father" in your human spirit; you become an heir – or siblings of Jesus, God's Son; and the Person of the Holy Spirit performs your adoption by infusing (or joining) your human spirit with God's Spirit. There is no need for an intellectual comprehension of the Trinity. You spiritually understand – or your human spirit is illuminated with God as a result of your salvation experience. The Bible says it is spiritually understood. "But the natural man does not receive the things of the Spirit of God, for they are foolishness to him; nor can he know them, because they are spiritually discerned" (1 Corinthians 2:14, NKJV). Romans 8:9-12 indicates that even though sin causes death as it did for Adam and Eve when they disobeyed God, you will live through faith in Christ Jesus. Through the power of the

Holy Spirit, you will experience God and understand the Trinity. John the Baptist encouraged doing works that are worthy of repentance (Matthew 3:8). Therefore, through the power of the Spirit, the deeds of sin in you can be put to death (Romans 8:13). The Trinity is understood by the new creature that you have become.

In conclusion, as we experience the three baptisms (repentance, salvation, and power), we have a revelation of the Trinity (Father, Son, and Holy Spirit). The salvation experience is not the human mind giving consent alone. It is a spiritual encounter through faith in the Messiah -- Jesus Christ. A relationship with God requires believing in Jesus. From there, the supernatural work of the Holy Spirit will create a new person with the power to be a witness that will bring others to faith in Jesus Christ.

BIBLE READING PLAN AND WORKSHEET

9th Month Bible Reading Assignment:

Instructions: Designate at least one hour daily to prayerfully read the following passages. Make the goal of completing the reading within the next thirty days: 2 Chronicles 29-32, 2 Kings 17-21, Isaiah 35-66, Hosea 1-14, Micah 1-7, Psalms 97-109, Proverbs 11-16, Matthew 24-28, Hebrews 1-13, and John 1-12.

Scriptural Review:

Instructions: Read each passage of scripture and write a short summary.

John 14:15-31

_____
_____
_____
_____

Matthew 3:13-17

_____
_____
_____
_____

Acts 19:1-3

_____
_____
_____
_____

Acts 19:4-7

_____
_____
_____
_____

Acts 1:1-8

_____
_____
_____
_____

Acts 2

_____
_____
_____
_____

Luke 3:7-20

_____
_____
_____
_____

Terminology Research

Instructions: Research and define each term. You may use a Bible dictionary or concordance and write a short summary.

Salvation

_____
_____
_____
_____

Holy Spirit

_____
_____
_____
_____

New Creation

_____
_____
_____
_____

Witness

_____
_____
_____
_____

Salvation and the Holy Spirit

Jerusalem

Judea

Samaria

Natural Man

Spiritual Man

John the Baptist

Water Baptism or Baptism of John

Speaking in Tongues

Prophesying

Notes:

CHAPTER 10

Worship God with Other Believers

"And let us consider one another in order to stir up love and good works, not forsaking the assembling of ourselves together, as is the manner of some, but exhorting one another, and so much the more as you see the Day approaching." (Hebrews 10:24-25, NIV)

Why is it important to attend church and worship God with other believers? It is indicated in this verse of Hebrews that Christians should gather to encourage each other in love and good works. However, this Bible study guide is being written in the middle of the COVID-19 pandemic that started in China at the end of 2019, and some churches are being asked and/or forced to close. As a result, many pastors have been broadcasting their church services on social media platforms like Facebook, YouTube, Twitter, Instagram, etc. But even before the pandemic, U.S. church membership and attendance had been dropping. Note, this statement reported by news.gallup.com:

> "U.S. church membership was 70% or higher from 1937 through 1976, falling modestly to an average of 68% in the 1970s through the 1990s…The past 20 years have seen an acceleration in the drop-off, with a 20-percentage-point decline since 1999 and more than half of that change occurring since the start of the current decade…The decline in church membership mostly reflects the fact that fewer Americans than in the past now have any religious affiliation. However, even

those who do identify with a particular religion are less likely to belong to a church or other place of worship than in the past." (Jones, 2019)

So, the questions we want to consider are: (1) Is it important for believers to meet together? and (2) If so, do they need to meet together in person? According to Hebrews 10:24-25, the answer to question one is yes. However, there is a growing number of people in the United States that no longer desire to attend church. In other nations, because the knowledge of the gospel is not as important or where there is strong persecution of believers, church attendance has always been a challenge and even dangerous. In many cases, meeting together – even the use of social media for religious purposes – is forbidden. Even in situations where believers are persecuted, they are more determined to meet together than those believers in the United States. According to the Bible, worshiping with other believers is needed to encourage, strengthen, and stir believers up to share and witness for the Gospel to be propagated to nonbelievers (Hebrews 10:24-25). However, because of social media, believers can still fellowship without meeting in person.

Why Worship God with Other Believers?

Whether believers are together in the same room or participating through social media, there are several reasons why believers should connect with each other in worshiping God. In this section, there are three reasons to consider: (1) to show love for one another, (2) to obtain spiritual growth and encouragement from one another, and (3) to celebrate God for who He is together.

(1) Show Love for One Another

The best way for believers to attract unbelievers to God is to display the love of God for one another. Jesus said, "By this everyone will know that you are my disciples, if you love one another" (John 13:35, NIV). In verse 34, He says for His disciples to love one another the way that He loved them. What does it look like for believers to love each other the way Jesus loves them? Here are some ways Jesus manifested His love for humanity, and these are the ways that we are to manifest our love for one another:

1. Love sacrificially (John 15:13)
2. Love unconditionally (1 Corinthians 13:4-7)
3. Love fearlessly (1 John 4:18)
4. Love covers others' faults (1 Peter 4:8)

The primary reason we have the Holy Spirit is to empower us to be witnesses of the generous gift of God's love. Jesus manifested the generosity of God when He sacrificed Himself. John 15:13 ESV says, "Greater love has no one than this, that someone lay down his life for his friends." We are not required to die on behalf of another, but we are expected to make the necessary sacrifices to serve and help others. I wonder if Americans have elected to stop attending church because many people have become selfish and self-centered. Some have made financial wealth synonymous with godliness: "They have lost their understanding of the truth. They think that devotion to God is a way to get rich" (I Timothy 6:5, ERV). They have become too busy with their pursuit of wealth that they no longer have time to attend church or pray with other believers. As you study the book of the Acts of the Apostles, you see believers in Jesus sharing their belongings, sharing a meal, and giving away their possessions (Acts 2:42-47). Church attendance can become mundane if there is no excitement about giving and being a blessing to others. The church should be more than a place to go to fulfill a sacred requirement. It is a place of sacrificing something for the benefit of others.

Our love must be unconditional as well. The Holy Spirit helps us to love difficult people and to love in difficult situations. The love of God in us never gives up, and it has endurance. "Love bears all things, believes all things, hopes all things, endures all things" (I Corinthians 13:7, ESV). Jesus' love produced hope for humanity, and He has already provided the ultimate sacrifice. How much more should we be willing to sacrifice some of what we have without restraints and with no regrets of not receiving anything in return?

Our love must be fearless. We see a great example of this with the Apostle Paul. He frequently suffered, but he was not discouraged by the hardships that he experienced. He said, "For the sake of Christ, then, I am content with weaknesses, insults, hardships, persecutions, and calamities. For when I am weak, then I am strong" (2 Corinthians 12:10, ESV). We can't allow difficulties of loving others to stop us from spreading the gospel and God's love. Fear – or being self-focused – keeps us from expressing the love of God. In reality, it brings into question the genuineness of our salvation, for "there is no fear in love, but perfect love casts out fear. For fear has to do with punishment, and whoever fears has not been perfected in love" (1 John 4:18, ESV).

Love empowers us to forgive others. "Most important of all, love each other deeply, because love makes you willing to forgive many sins" (1 Peter 4:8, ERV). Like Jesus, we must be able to overlook the faults of others in order to give and serve them sacrificially, unconditionally, and fearlessly. Unforgiveness distorts the love of God and prevents us from reflecting the new creation we have become through Jesus Christ. It counteracts the work of forgiveness that we have received. Because of Adam and Eve, we all have sins. Believers' sins have been forgiven and our assignment is to help unregenerate people come and experience the forgiveness that we have received. When unbelievers see believers loving each other and forgiving one another, they can be convinced of the love God has for them.

(2) Spiritual Growth and Encouragement

The practice of followers of God meeting together didn't start with Jesus and His Church. As far back as in the Old Testament, we can find the assembly of the Jewish people to worship God, as indicated here in Nehemiah 8:1:

> "... all the people came together as one in the square before the Water Gate. They told Ezra the teacher of the Law to bring out the Book of the Law of Moses, which the Lord had commanded for Israel." (NIV)

The Jews in Jesus' time were still gathering in the synagogues. Many passages like Luke 4:16-47 describe Jesus speaking to them and teaching them in synagogues. Ephesians 4 explains how Jesus gave special training abilities (or gifts) to Apostles, Prophets, Pastors, Teachers, and Evangelists to help people grow spiritually so that the Body of Christ (the Church that Jesus started) would have unity in the spreading of the gospel. The gifts were to edify and encourage believers and to help them stay strong in their faith in Jesus Christ. To have access to these gifts, you must be connected with a church where they are operating or training others with them. Also, you may have one or more of these gifts and others need to be edified by you. "For just as each of us has one body with many members, and these members do not all have the same function, so in Christ, we, though many, form one body, and each member belongs to all the others" (Romans 12:4-5, NIV). We cannot benefit from each other's gifts unless we have contact with each other. Therefore, it is important for believers to fellowship so that they can help each other grow and be strong in sharing the gospel with unbelievers.

(3) Celebrate God for Who He Is Together

In Nehemiah 8, the people worshiped and celebrated God as the great God. They did some of the things that are seen practiced in church gatherings all over the world today.

> Ezra opened the book. All the people could see him because he was standing above them; and as he opened it, the people all stood up. Ezra praised the Lord, the great God; and all the people lifted their hands and responded, "Amen! Amen!" Then they bowed down and worshiped the Lord with their faces to the ground. (Nehemiah 8: 5-6, NIV)

The leader, Ezra, was high above as he read the Law from the book, and the people praised the Lord by shouting, "Amen!" They stood as the leader read and bowed with their faces to the ground to worship God. Other times, when people worshiped, they announced that God was the great God over all other gods. "For the Lord is the great God, the great King above all gods" (Psalm 95:5, NIV). It is an essential practice for believers to celebrate God and declare His greatness as one voice. When unbelievers come to church and see believers united in worshiping God, this attracts them to put their hope in Jesus Christ for salvation.

These are a few passages from the Bible that promote the reasons that it is important for believers to worship God together with other believers. Modern technology and social media have enabled many of these worship practices to continue even when churches closed during the COVID-19 pandemic. Believers were able to connect without being in the same place or building. The Church of Jesus Christ will continue to thrive as believers connect frequently. If possible, in the same room, but many have discovered that they can still be involved in church fellowship through social media platforms. They can bring their gifts as well as receive ministry from others.

BIBLE READING PLAN AND WORKSHEET

10th Month Bible Reading Assignment:

Instructions: Designate at least one hour daily to prayerfully read the following passages. Make the goal of completing the reading within the next thirty days: 2 Chronicles 33-36:1-10, 2 Kings 22-25, Jeremiah 1-24, Daniel 1-12, Ezekiel 1-8, Zephaniah 1-7, Nahum 1-3, Habakkuk 1-3, Psalms 110-121, Proverbs 17-21, Mark 1, James 1-5, John 13-21, 1 Peter 1-5, 2 Peter 1-3, 1 John 1-5, 2 John 1, 3 John 1, and Jude 1.

Scriptural Review:

Instructions: Read each passage of scripture and write a short summary.

Ephesians 4

_____

_____

_____

_____

Romans 12

_____

_____

_____

_____

Nehemiah 8

_____

_____

_____

_____

Terminology Research

Instructions: Research and define each term. You may use a Bible dictionary or concordance and write a short summary.

Synagogues

_____

_____

_____

_____

Water Gate

_____

_____

_____

_____

Book of the Law of Moses

_____

_____

_____

_____

Twelves Gates of Jerusalem

_____

_____

_____

_____

Worship God with Other Believers

Body of Christ

Notes:

CHAPTER 11

The Believer's Role in the Church Jesus Started

"Praising God and having favor with all the people. And the Lord added to the church daily those who were being saved."

(Acts 2:47, NKJV)

It was mentioned in Chapter 10 that people's interest in religion or attending church has decreased in the United States. In other countries, however, there are many people that still value attending church even if they are persecuted for it. From the time Jesus started the Church, there has been opposition to Christians gathering to worship God and learn of the work of Jesus to save the world. Believers or Christians all over the world must continue to be involved in Jesus' church – even if it is no longer popular, or if there is opposition and persecution. Believers have been commissioned to deliver the gospel of Jesus Christ (the good news of His salvation) to the world. When Jesus was speaking to His disciples while meeting with them after His resurrection, He gave this commission found in Matthew 28:16-20:

> Then the eleven disciples went away into Galilee, to the mountain which Jesus had appointed for them. When they saw Him, they worshiped Him; but some doubted. And Jesus came and spoke to them, saying, "All authority has been given to Me in heaven and on earth. Go therefore and make disciples of all the nations, baptizing them in the name of the Father and of the Son and of the Holy Spirit, teaching them to observe all things

that I have commanded you; and lo, I am with you always, even to the end of the age." (NKJV)

In this chapter, we will cover the believer's role in the church that Jesus started. There are four assignments mentioned my Jesus in Matthew 28:16-20: (1) worship Jesus Christ, (2) go and make Him disciples of all humanity, (3) baptize believers in His name (Father, Son, and Holy Spirit), and (4) teach believers to keep His commandments.

(1) Worship Jesus Christ

What is worship? In Matthew 3:17, God from heaven said of Jesus Christ, "And a voice from heaven said, "This is my dearly loved Son, who brings me great joy" (NIV). If God recognizes the divinity of Jesus Christ, how much more are believers to worship Jesus Christ before others in the world? In John 12:32, Jesus said, "And I, if I be lifted up from the earth, will draw all men unto me" ((KJV). The role of the believer is to lift up – or worship – Jesus Christ. Worshiping Jesus Christ as God draws people to follow God and encourages their faith to receive salvation. Also, when believers worship Jesus Christ, great joy is expressed. This experience of joy can be felt by unbelievers when they are at church or at other places where believers are worshiping Jesus Christ. I remember visiting a church service as an unbeliever and experiencing God's presence as Christians worshiped Jesus Christ in songs and music. When I believed in Jesus Christ, I continued experiencing this joy in a personal way. I had never experienced this kind of joy in my life before. This experience was Jesus' Baptism to Salvation that was discussed in Chapter 9. When believers worship Jesus Christ at church, visitors can sense His presence, and in the same way that I was saved, others will be saved as well.

(2) Go and Make Disciples of all Humanity

The second assignment of believers is to make disciples of all nations. Believers remain on the earth to help bring unbelievers to salvation in Jesus Christ. Note that Jesus was resurrected to Heaven, but His followers were not. Jesus' followers were left on the earth with the job of making more disciples of Jesus Christ from people living in all nations of the world. What is a disciple? Billy Graham gives this meaning:

> "What does it mean to be a disciple of Jesus? It means first of all that we want to learn from him — and we will, as we study God's word, the Bible, and listen to others teach from it. Make the Bible part of your life every day. The Psalmist said, 'The unfolding of your words gives light; it gives understanding to the simple'" (Psalm 119:130). (Graham, 2019)

Disciples learn the Bible and teach it to others. By doing so, they are making disciples of anyone who believes what they teach; or, they are creating a community where people can come and obtain salvation. In that community, the Bible is studied and those converted through Jesus' Baptism to Salvation are made disciples, who then make more disciples. The role of believers in the church that Jesus started is to be a disciple and make more disciples.

(3) Baptize Believers

In John's Baptism, three names or Persons of God are mentioned: Father, Son, and the Holy Spirit. Plus, Jesus said to baptize in My name and not names: "baptizing them in the name of the Father and of the Son and of the Holy Spirit" (Matthew 28:19, NKJV). These three Persons of God have been confusing to people for many years. It is a cause of contention between Christian and Muslim believers. Both religions teach that God is one deity, but Christianity has God as three Persons: Father, Son, and Holy Spirit (known as the Trinity). Whereas Muslims don't like that idea. So, what do the three Persons of God – or the Trinity – mean in baptizing believers? Jesus Christ is the embodiment of the oneness of God that is expressed in the Trinity. He possessed God's trilogy as a human being when He was on Earth. "For in Christ lives all the fullness of God in a human body" (Colossians 2:9, NLT). God's trilogy in whole has three Persons – Father, Son, and Holy Spirit – which are all present in the Person of Jesus Christ. When someone believes in Jesus Christ, they supernaturally become a new creation, or experiences Jesus' Baptism to Salvation. They experience the Trinity of God in Jesus Christ, who is the fullness of God.

In the Trinity, the three Persons of God are living within believers, and their humanity can now relate to God in the same way Adam and Eve did in the Garden before their disobedience. Jesus Christ, in a human body, manifested God's generosity to all of humanity as He walked the earth with His disciples. Now, when a person believes in Jesus Christ and receives salvation (freedom from the penalty of death that was received as a result of the disobedience of Adam and Eve), the fullness of God enters them in the Person of

Jesus Christ. Usually, the next step that is encouraged is water baptism or John's Baptism as discussed in Chapter 9.

The believer's role in the church is to baptize people in water once they have been baptized with Jesus' salvation, or when people are born again by the power of the Holy Spirit. Water baptism is an important Church practice. Believers (primarily pastors) baptize new believers in the name of the Father, Son, and Holy Spirit. Jesus said that He had to be water baptized to fulfill all righteousness (Matthew 3:15). If Jesus had to be water baptized, all believers with the fullness of God need to be water baptized as well. To have another believer or a pastor available to baptize you, it is important to be a member of a church or be in fellowship with another believer so that you can be baptized. Water baptism is a testimony to others of your commitment to be a follower of Jesus Christ.

(4) Teach Believers to Keep Jesus' Command

The believer's role in the church is to teach disciples to keep Jesus' command: "teaching them to observe all things that I have commanded you" (Matthew 28:20, NKJV). What was Jesus' command? What is it that His disciples are to observe? While on Earth, Jesus demonstrated His ministry of reconciliation. The Bible says God was in Christ reconciling the world to Himself (2 Corinthians 5:19). In giving the commission in Matthew 28, He was conferring His assignment to His disciples, which is to keep Jesus' commandment to make other disciples. Jesus' commandment to His disciples is to make other disciples, or to do the work of reconciling unbelievers of all nations to God through Jesus.

According to 2 Corinthians 5:18-21, believers have been given the assignment of helping others be reconciled to God.

> All this is from God, who reconciled us to himself through Christ and gave us the ministry of reconciliation: that God was reconciling the world to himself in Christ, not counting people's sins against them. And he has committed to us the message of reconciliation. We are therefore Christ's ambassadors, as though God were making his appeal through us. We implore you on Christ's behalf: Be reconciled to God. God made him who had no sin to be sin for us so that in him we might become the righteousness of God. (NIV)

We have studied that during the disobedience of Adam and Eve, their sinful nature was passed to all humanity. The work of Jesus Christ in the world was to pave the way for humanity to come into a relationship with God again. When believers obey Jesus' commandment to teach all nations to follow His teachings, unbelievers become reconciled to God when they believe the gospel. Unbelievers cannot know what Jesus Christ has done unless they hear the gospel being proclaimed.

> How, then, can they call on the one they have not believed in? And how can they believe in the one of whom they have not heard? And how can they hear without someone preaching to them? And how can anyone preach unless they are sent? As it is written: "How beautiful are the feet of those who bring good news!" (Romans 10:14-15, NIV)

Ministry of Reconciliation

The role of believers in the Church is to ensure that the gospel is proclaimed to all people and all nations of the world. Also, it is important for believers to attend and be involved in the church that Jesus started. There is an indication that Jesus Christ intended that believers should work together in helping people be reconciled in their relationship with God. We will call this the Ministry of Reconciliation. By selecting Apostles, and by the fact that Jesus Christ had many people following Him from city to city to help Him preach, He had plans to have His followers continue His Ministry of Reconciliation. Here is a record of Jesus sending His disciples out to preach: "And He called the twelve to Himself, and began to send them out two by two, and gave them power over unclean spirits" (Mark 6:7 NKJV). The Apostles and followers of Jesus were engaged (at the start of the church that Jesus built) in spreading the gospel and making disciples. Therefore, before His death and resurrection, and afterwards, Jesus' ultimate goal was for believers to have a community to work together and not independently of the other members of the church!

BIBLE READING PLAN AND WORKSHEET

11th Month Bible Reading Assignment:

Instructions: Designate at least one hour daily to prayerfully read the following passages. Make the goal of completing the reading within the next thirty days: 2 Chronicles 36:11-21, Jeremiah 25-39, Ezekiel 9-48, Psalms 122-136, Proverbs 22-26, Mark 2-16, and Revelation 1-15.

Scriptural Review:

Instructions: Read each passage of scripture and write a short summary.

Ephesians 4

_____

_____

_____

_____

Matthew 28:16-20

_____

_____

_____

_____

Matthew 3:17

_____

_____

_____

_____

Psalm 119:130

_____
_____
_____
_____

Colossians 2:9

_____
_____
_____
_____

2 Corinthians 5:19

_____
_____
_____
_____

Terminology Research

Instructions: Research and define each term. You may use a Bible dictionary or concordance and write a short summary.

The Believer's Role in the Church Jesus Started

Commandment(s)

_____

_____

_____

_____

Reconciliation

_____

_____

_____

_____

Ministry

_____

_____

_____

_____

Ministry of Reconciliation

_____

_____

_____

_____

Trinity

_____
_____
_____
_____

Oneness

_____
_____
_____
_____

Disciple

_____
_____
_____
_____

Christianity

_____
_____
_____
_____

Notes:

CHAPTER 12

The Church's Role in the World

"These were his instructions to them: "The harvest is great, but the workers are few. So pray to the Lord who is in charge of the harvest; ask him to send more workers into his fields." (Luke 10:2, NLT)

Jesus is sending His followers to harvest lives into His kingdom. This seems to be a shift in focus from just Israel. However, the nation of Israel continued to be the evidence of the connection of God with people in the earth long after Jesus' coming, death, and resurrection. Through Abraham, the nation was called long ago to be set apart from other nations to be God's chosen people (Genesis 18:18, NKJV). The prevailing existence of Israel is still a reality because there is hardly a month that goes by that this nation isn't mentioned as God's special people. Abraham's descendants (the people of Israel) were identified, in essence, as how the Messiah or Christ would come and through Him all the nations of the world would be blessed (Genesis 18:18, KJV). Meaning, Israel as a nation, was born biblically through the covenant made by God with Abraham. This was covered in Chapter 8. With Jesus, things seem to have changed. According to Jesus, His followers are being identified as God's people, and He is bringing salvation to both Jews and Gentiles. In this chapter's key verse, Luke 10:2, believers in Him are given the commission to make disciples of all men from every nation. In other words, everybody can become God's special chosen people. "But you are a chosen generation, a royal priesthood, a holy nation, His own special people, that you may proclaim the praises of Him who called you out of darkness into His marvelous light" (1 Peter 2:9, KJV).

Although Israel is still being highlighted in the world as God's nation, the church that Jesus started (which includes Jews and Gentiles) is the tool that God is using to deliver the message of salvation through faith in Him. The role of the Church in the world is to be the mouthpiece of God on the earth to all of humanity. This assignment of the Church is to be delivered to unchurched people – both Jews (or Israelites) and Gentiles (all other nations of the world). In Chapter 11 of this guide, it is recorded that Billy Graham noted the importance of disciples learning from Jesus Christ so that they can make more disciples of Jesus Christ. In addition to making disciples, the Church has been left by Jesus Christ in the world to be His testimony or witness.

There are three principal ways the Church can be a witness to the world: (1) be in the world but separate, (2) show God's image to the world, and (3) show God's love to one another and others.

Be Separate from the World

One verse in the Bible puts it this way: "Therefore, come out from among unbelievers, and separate yourselves from them, says the Lord. Don't touch their filthy things, and I will welcome you" (2 Corinthians 6:17, NLT). Jesus explains this to His disciples by telling them that they are in the world but not of the world (John 15:19-22, NLT). Sin had the power to distort God's image through Adam and Eve, as indicated in Genesis 3. It is important that believers live

The Church's Role in the World

differently from the world to disconnect from any temptation to practice sin. Being intimate (or closely acquainted) with people of the world that promote the practice of sin as acceptable, produces an appetite in believers for sin.

> Do not love this world nor the things it offers you, for when you love the world, you do not have the love of the Father in you. For the world offers only a craving for physical pleasure, a craving for everything we see, and pride in our achievements and possessions. These are not from the Father but are from this world. And this world is fading away, along with everything that people crave. But anyone who does what pleases God will live forever. (1 John 2:15-17, NLT)

The lifestyle of a believer should be distinct from the practices of unbelievers when it comes to the changed life that John the Baptist encouraged. As a result of repentance and salvation, believers live their lives separately or differently from that of unbelievers. For example, they do not participate in sex before marriage, nor do they have same-gender marital relationships. In Ephesians 5, there is a liturgy (Christian worship or practices) of observances that believers perform that many nonbelievers may see as foolish or unnecessary. But for the church to fulfill its role in the world as being a witness, the lifestyle standards set in Ephesians 5 cannot be ignored by believers.

Being separate is more than just avoiding the sinful practices of unbelievers. Jesus spoke of a Kingdom in which He is King. This Kingdom is different from the world in which unbelievers function. The only people in this Kingdom are believers in Jesus Christ. This Kingdom exists now alongside the worldly systems, and it will continue to exist when Jesus Christ returns (and afterwards) to occupy the Earth with His followers (Revelations 21, NKJV). Below are a few descriptions of what this Kingdom is all about with scriptural references:

1. The Kingdom brings salvation and healing (Matthew 4:23, NKJV)
2. The Kingdom brings Good News (Matthew 9:35, NKJV)
3. The Kingdom produces a better lifestyle than that of the Law (Matthew 5:20, NKJV)
4. The Kingdom cannot be defeated by any enemy (Matthew 11:12, NKJV)
5. The Kingdom has power over unclean spirits (Matthew 12:28, NKJV)
6. The Kingdom is near to anyone who believes (Matthew 12:28, NKJV)

Show God's Image to the World

The Church is an entity set apart from the world with the purpose of standing out distinguishably different from other people in the world. When Jesus' church displays God's image, the purpose for which God created Adam and Eve in the Garden of Eden becomes unveiled. God wants humanity to see Him in a personal way. However, He intends for His church to introduce Him to people outside of His Kingdom and give them an unforgettable experience. In Matthew 5:13-16, Jesus teaches that His disciples are to be flavorful like salt.

> You are the salt of the earth. But if the salt loses its saltiness, how can it be made salty again? It is no longer good for

anything, except to be thrown out and trampled underfoot. You are the light of the world. A town built on a hill cannot be hidden. Neither do people light a lamp and put it under a bowl. Instead they put it on its stand, and it gives light to everyone in the house. In the same way, let your light shine before others, that they may see your good deeds and glorify your Father in heaven. (NIV)

If the light and image of God is to be shown, Jesus' followers are the ones to display it. When we are salt that makes others salty for God, we are fulfilling the commission of increasing the number of laborers in the harvest field.

Show God's Love to One Another and Others

The Church is called to love people within it (1 John 4:20, NIV) and those that are not members of the congregation of believers. God is love. He loves everybody, and He wants His followers to love people. As His children, we are commanded to exemplify love for all humanity. John 13:35 says, "By this all will know that you are My disciples, if you have love for one another" (NKJV). Also, Matthew 5:43-45 has this admonishment:

> You have heard that it was said, 'You shall love your neighbor and hate your enemy.' But I say to you, love your enemies, bless those who curse you, do good to those who hate you, and pray for those who spitefully use you and persecute you, that you may be sons of your Father in heaven; for He makes His sun rise on the evil and on the good, and sends rain on the just and on the unjust. (NKJV)

Even when the Church is hated by the world, it is encouraged to love all of humanity. Through the church that Jesus started, God reveals Himself. He has the power to reveal Himself to mere human beings as He did for Simon Bar-Jonah (Matthew 16:13-20, NKJV). God has Jesus' Body (the Church) as His witness on the earth. There is One Body with many members.

When unbelievers encounter a member of this Church, they encounter Christ. An encounter with Christ is an encounter with God. It is the Holy Spirit (Who is also God) within believers that reveals the image of God to unbelievers. Mere "flesh and blood" has no power to do so. The Church is God manifesting His love through Jesus Christ to the world. "For God so loved the world that He gave His only begotten Son, that whoever believes in Him should not perish but have everlasting life" (John 3:16, NKJV). There is a supernatural manifestation of the generosity of God in the Person of Jesus Christ inside believers. This is known as being born again – or salvation. This manifestation of the image of God is in people who believe in Jesus Christ all over the world because God is sending His laborers to harvest in this vast field of humanity. Now, the laborers are no longer few.

BIBLE READING PLAN AND WORKSHEET

12th Month Bible Reading Assignment:

Instructions: Designate at least one hour daily to prayerfully read the following passages. Make the goal of completing the reading within the next thirty days: 2 Chronicles 36:22-23, Jeremiah 40-52, Lamentations 1-5, Ezra 1-10, Haggai 1-2, Zechariah 1-14, Esther 1-10,

Nehemiah 1-13, Malachi 1-4, Psalms 137-150, Proverbs 27-31, Luke 1-24, and Revelations 16-22.

Scriptural Review:

Instructions: Read each passage of scripture and write a short summary.

2 Corinthians 6:15-18

_____
_____
_____
_____

Matthew 5:13-16

_____
_____
_____
_____

John 15:19-22

_____
_____
_____
_____

The Church's Role in the World

John 13:33-35

_____
_____
_____
_____

Ephesians 5

_____
_____
_____
_____

Terminology Research

    Instructions: Research and define each term. You may use a Bible dictionary or concordance and write a short summary.

Witness

_____
_____
_____
_____

Testimony

God's Image

Separate from the World

One Body

Notes:

CONCLUSION

The intent of this manual, Jesus the Manifested Generosity of God, is to provide a tool to help with studying and understanding the plan of God to redeem humanity. Many believe that Jesus' existence started on Earth. Jesus Christ is God Who became flesh to redeem humanity by destroying the power of sin over people's lives by His death and resurrection. God does not have a beginning, and His existence is eternal. God created the heavens and the earth to place man in to fulfill His mission to express His glory to all of humanity for all of eternity. The first man, Adam/Eve, had the image of God their Creator before sin. After they disobeyed God, that image became distorted. Jesus Christ – God in humanity with us or "Immanuel" – came to restore humanity with the ability to reflect Himself as He intended from the beginning. When humanity believes in Jesus Christ as the savior of the world, they will become restored to the eternal nature of God. Not everyone will believe what has been presented in this manual. Nonetheless, the goal is to help those who believe convince others that Jesus Christ is God's generosity and mercy to the world.

WORKS CITED

Deffinbaugh, B (2004). "32. The Tabernacle, the Dwelling Place of God (Exodus 36:8-39:43)." 32. The Tabernacle, the Dwelling Place of God (Exodus 36:8-39:43) | Bible.org, bible.org/seriespage/32-tabernacle-dwelling-place-god-exodus-368-3943.

Jones, Jeffrey M. "U.S. Church Membership Down Sharply in Past Two Decades." Gallup.com, Gallup, 23 Nov. 2020, news.gallup.com/poll/248837/church-membership-down-sharply-past-two-decades.aspx.

Kansas City, and BILLY GRAHAM Tribune Media Services. "Billy Graham: What Does It Mean to Be a Disciple of Jesus?" Kansas City, The Kansas City Star, www.kansascity.com/living/liv-columns-blogs/billy-graham/article77272832.html.

"Keyword Search: Church." BibleGateway, www.biblegateway.com/quicksearch/?qs_version=KJV&quicksearch=church&startnumber=1.

Schrock, David, et al. "How Is Jesus a Prophet Like Moses?" The Gospel Coalition, 13 June 2020, www.thegospelcoalition.org/article/jesus-prophet-moses/.

ADDITIONAL RESOURCES

Bible Reading Plan

This manuscript used the plan provided by Victory Christian Center in Tulsa, Oklahoma. You can find this plan by searching "Victory App" in the App Store, or you can download a plan here: https://bibleproject.com/downloads/reading-plan/. Plus, I like this Bible Gateway tool: https://www.biblegateway.com/. It doesn't matter which Bible reading plan you decide to use! What's important is that you start reading and studying the Bible for yourself. I believe for too long people have depended on others, especially clergy, to find the truth about Jesus Christ. By doing this, you will discover God's generous gift, Jesus Christ, as your personal Friend and Savior. Firsthand revelation is better than relying on someone else to pray and be with God for you – like they do in other religious practices. You will hear the gospel as you travel through the pages from Genesis to Revelation. Faith will arise in your heart, and the Holy Spirit will make you into a totally new person.

Use a Bible Dictionary and/or Concordance

I strongly recommend new believers or beginners in studying scriptures to invest in a Bible Dictionary or Concordance if one is not included in the Bible you use. Here are some resources that have been helpful to me in my pursuit of understanding the story of Jesus in the Bible:

1. Holman Christian Standard Bible: Dictionary and Concordance of the Holy Bible

2. The Hebrew-Greek Key Study Bible (includes Lexicon to the Old and New Testaments plus a Hebrew and Chaldee Dictionary)
3. Strong's Exhaustive Concordance by James Strong

Because we are in the age of technology, we have easy access to Bibles and study materials online or through various apps which are free to download to your phone or computer. Many of these tools are at your fingertips. If you can't afford to buy or have technology readily available, your local library has a wealth of free resources to help you study the Bible. We have hope of you encountering the Savior of the world and that you will become a part of the church that Jesus started. Most importantly, you will share Jesus, the Manifested Generosity of God with everyone you meet!

www.ingramcontent.com/pod-product-compliance
Lightning Source LLC
LaVergne TN
LVHW021818060526
838201LV00058B/3430